The Outspoken Ones

THE OUTSPOKEN ONES

*Twelve Prophets of Israel
and Juda*

by DOM HUBERT VAN ZELLER

SHEED & WARD · NEW YORK

2 2 4
V 3 9 0

Sackcloth and Ashes

Watch and Pray

Manufactured in the United States of America

CONTENTS

The Kingdoms of Israel and Juda

THE Israelites were one kingdom, under Saul, David and Solomon, till 937 B.C.

After Solomon's death, the kingdom divided into two—the Northern, Israel, ruled by various dynasties; the Southern, Juda, ruled by the line of David. Juda contained the tribes of Juda and Benjamin and a large part of Simeon and Dan. Israel had the remaining eight tribes.

Israel lasted for just over two hundred years, till it was conquered by the Assyrians in 722 B.C.

Juda continued another century and a half, until 586 B.C., when Jerusalem surrendered to the Babylonians and its king Sedecias and most of the people were taken away to Babylon. Persia conquered Babylon, and in 538 B.C. there was a beginning of return from exile.

Judea was ruled in turn by Persia and Egypt. In 198 B.C. Antiochus the Great of Syria defeated the Ptolemies and took Palestine. A savage persecution of the Jewish religion began under Antiochus IV Epiphanes; a revolt led by the Macchabees overthrew the Syrians and led to an independent Jewish kingdom which lasted the best part of a century, till Jerusalem fell to the Romans in 63 B.C.

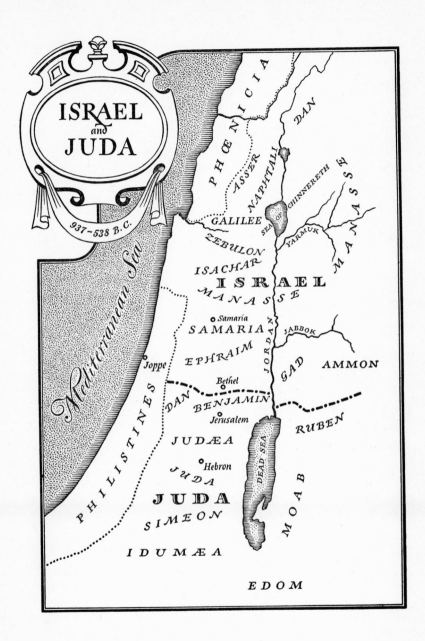

PREFACE

Biblical studies, like Biblical characters, have their moods. Until quite recently there was next to nothing that one could read about the Minor Prophets; today there is a good deal. Commentaries and histories abound. Twenty years ago, when the essays which are gathered together into this book were written, so few Catholic scholars were showing interest in the Prophets that the authorities cited had perforce to be those of the Anglican or Hebrew tradition. I mention this because a reviewer of one of my books which has been reprinted in America took exception not long ago to the sources which I had drawn upon in my work. But at the time of writing there had been hardly any other. Rather than re-write the whole twelve sketches, basing my exposition upon recent Catholic investigation, I have decided to confine the task of revision to the clarification of phrases, the elimination of redundancies (and, where I have discovered them, errors), the furbishing of syntax and punctuation. So slight and personal is the portraiture that this course has seemed justifiable: the historical setting plays only a ministering role: the main thing is the spiritual content. And this brings me to a further point. Conjectural though much of the material is, the stories which follow are not fairy stories. Where I have speculated I have said quite clearly that I was speculating: these biographies are not little pious novels. All along I have tried to keep the strictly spiritual, and sometimes the strictly mystical, purpose before my mind. Just enough of what I conceived to be scientific apparatus has been dragged in to give authority to the narrative, and no more. It is easy to make errors of judgment about this. Exegesis, to the lay reader, goes a long way. And it is to the lay reader, rather than to the professional Scripture student, that this book about the Minor Prophets is addressed. If the candidate for examination gets something he can use, so much the better. The kind of person whom I am trying to cater for, however, is the casual reader who has a shrewd guess that there is more in the Bible than ever came out of it—and who wants to do a little deep-sea diving on his own. It is the amateur whom we want to catch and interest. Certainly he will find, as the writer has found, that there is nothing so rewarding and exciting as hunting for the shapes of things under the surface of the inspired word of God.

SACKCLOTH AND ASHES

I. Osee: The Lover

i

'THE word of the Lord that came to Osee the son of Beeri, in the days of Ozias, Joathan, Achaz, and Ezechias, kings of Juda, and in the days of Jeroboam the son of Joas, king of Israel.' So runs the opening verse of what is the longest as well as perhaps the most melancholy of the Books which come from those whom we call, on account only of the brevity of their writings, the Minor Prophets.

About Beeri, Osee's father, nothing whatever is known and tradition is silent regarding the prophet's early years. In fact tradition has proved singularly reticent where the whole of Osee's life is concerned, confining itself to the solitary piece of information—and that the merest legend—to the effect that the prophet died a prisoner in Babylon and was brought back for burial in Palestine where he was venerated for generations by the sons of the people whom he had denounced.[1] If there is nothing to be learned from his own pen or from local history of Osee's upbringing, certainly the other Books of the Bible furnish nothing more. For the 'life' of this prophet we have precisely three chapters to go upon—the three autobiographical chapters at the beginning—but the events which these chapters record are so revealing that our picture of the man and our understand-

[1] Even up till the end of the fourth century A.D. there appear to have been at least two places at which the supposed body of Osee was visited by pilgrims.

ing of his message are by no means as incomplete as one might be led to expect from the slimness of the data. Osee emerges at the end of it a heroic if pathetic figure, saddened and chastened and bewildered, not knowing where he stands in the sight of God and completely at sea about himself and his mission as a prophet, yet to us presenting a clear-cut personality, rich and radiant with hope, and all the more living for the intimacy of the information he supplies.

In telling us that Jeroboam was king of Israel when the word of God first came to him, Osee makes it fairly easy for us to get the lie of the land at the time of his appearance in the rôle of a prophet. It is Jeroboam the Second of whom he speaks, the great-grandson of Jehu who had been the first of that house to sit upon the throne of Israel. Jeroboam's grandfather, Joachaz, and his father, Joas, had increased the power of the Northern Kingdom during their reigns of seventeen and sixteen years respectively, but it was not until his own rule was well under way that Israel's zenith of prosperity was reached. The period of triumph, however, was destined to be short-lived, for the moral decline which it was the work of the prophets Osee and Amos to expose seems to have reached bedrock in the ill-starred reign of Zacharias, some fifty years before the final doom. This too it had been the work of Osee and Amos to proclaim. Zacharias was Jeroboam's son; he lived to enjoy only six turbulent months of kingship before he was killed by his guests at a dinner party. The murder of Zacharias and the murders of his immediate successors took place in the regions of 770 or a little later. Hebrew chronology is perplexing, especially when, as here in the case of Osee's opening verses, two lines of kings are given—those of Israel as well as those of Juda—and where the parallel dates appear to disagree. The date problem, however, need not trouble us if we remember that Osee was a Northerner writing for Northerners, and that the reigns of Juda's kings interested him not at all. He may easily have made a mistake about who was on the throne in the South at the time of his hearing the word of the Lord, but there could be no doubt as to who was ruling in Israel; Jeroboam the son of Joas was not a sovereign to be confused with any other.

As to the exact place on the map where the prophet poured out his maledictions, it would be rash to pin him down to any one city; Bethel seems to find favour with the commentators who do so, but since Osee writes with equal familiarity of many other cities in Samaria, and since it is unlikely that two prophets, Osee *and* Amos, almost contemporaries, should have chosen to make the same spot their centre, we are not obliged to regard the people of Bethel as either deserving or receiving such undistributed obloquy. Bethel was certainly the scene of Amos' activities, but of that later. The towns of the Northern Kingdom are lumped together in Osee's mind, and he refers to them collectively as 'Ephraim'; the probability seems to be that he passed from one to another prophesying the dissolution. The message was not to any one city, nor did he fulminate against any one abuse; the decadence he objected to and the fall he heralded were of general application, and it seems much more likely that he delivered his threats while on the road. Violent reactionaries are seldom suffered to become residents of any long standing. Osee's home when Gomer was with him—if the term 'home' can be applied at all in that connexion—may well have been in Bethel, but then his prophecies for the most part, as we shall see, are believed to have been delivered in that lady's absence.

Perhaps this is the best place, before recounting the drama of Osee's married life, to say that the incidental passages—those that refer to what appears to be directly historical matter or to personal reminiscence—will be taken in this sketch to have been meant literally. As Scripture, the Prophecy of Osee owes its main interest and value to its 'typical' character (thus the prophet's relations with his wife may be taken *simply* as referring to the Lord's dealing with the unfaithful people of Israel), but as narrative apart from anything else the book has its significance, and it is in this capacity that Osee provides the substance of the following pages. Without entering, then, into the question as to whether the prophet's 'powerful heart story' was a dream or a dramatic reality, a fancy or a fact, we examine what the man actually wrote and draw our conclusions from that. The application of symbolism in the Scriptures must be left to the Church; mere moralization, however, and tentative reconstruction may be undertaken by the humblest of her sons, and it is in such a spirit of submission that we presume to embark upon our Minor Prophetical study. Thus if Osee's matrimonial affairs are, in fact, no more than a parable, we can at least examine its setting and draw a conclusion from its import.

ii

'And the Lord said to Osee: Go, take thee a wife of fornications, and have of her children of fornication; for the land by fornication shall depart from the Lord.' The young prophet obeyed at once, 'he went, and took Gomer the daughter of Debelaim,' and from that moment the sorrows of Osee begin.

Considering that the union was to darken the rest of Osee's private life and colour his public utterances, it is significant to notice that there is never so much as a hint in the whole book that he resented the Divine injunction, though it must have been perfectly obvious to him—at all events in retrospect and until the final dawn had come—that, left to himself, he could have made a very much happier match. It is possible that Osee realized in a dim sort of way even at the outset that to 'miss one's vocation' might conceivably be a vocation in itself. God seems to call some people to make what humanly speaking are the mistakes of a lifetime in order that the sufferings resulting from such decisions may constitute the essence of a deeper vocation altogether. Certainly, whether Osee was able to see this or not, it seems to have been what actually happened in his case. Here he was, bound irrevocably to an altogether unworthy wife in the fixed belief that it was God's will that he should be so bound; his marriage would cause him endless miseries; he was to wish for the rest of his working life that he could be free of his duties as a husband; Gomer was for ever to be the big distraction, the harassing preoccupation of the man's mind; she would interfere—if only by her absence and the duties which that absence would impose—with his work of preaching and teaching the word of God; she would rob him of the peace and time that he would have wished for prayer; she would come, in effect—so it would seem to him—between his soul and God. Another thing: Osee loved his wife despite the woman's wantonness. Imagine the man's feelings: how could he possibly—caught as he was in the toils of human longings—pretend to the heart-free vocation of the man of God? How could he give to God while what he had to give was Gomer's right? Were not the words of the Lord perhaps illusion, and his passion real—the only reality?

Such, then, was the nature of Osee's early honeymoon years,

and it was from out of this tragic and all but embittering medley that God drew the satisfaction He sought for in His servant. Had the prophet been allowed to do what he must surely have wished again and again that he had done, and pursued a way of life according to his pious inclinations, there might conceivably have been a prophecy, and there might even have been one more pattern of virtue at the end of it all, but there would never have been a prophecy with just that note of pain, or a saint and prophet with just that spirit of darkened but glowing hope. It is as if God purposed to Himself two things: first that a book should be found in His Writ that was to proclaim His Mercy and His Love before any other of His attributes; and second that a prophet should be raised up to write that book in the scorching tears of his own shame. Thus it was necessary that an adulterous wife should teach the lesson that no amount of abstract theory would do. Osee's 'reaction' to Gomer's infidelity, chastisement, and return, won for him at long last an insight into the infinite tenderness of God.

Postulating some such design in the mind of God, the words of Osee's second verse, 'take thee a wife of fornications,' are not as incongruous as they might seem. The Lord has said as much to others of His friends. Never, it must be insisted, in such cases is it a question of sin or imperfection that is commanded; never even is the injunction against the *nature* (in the sense of 'personality,' 'temperament,' etc.) of the one commanded, but only against his better judgment; and lastly, never does the order involve the hurt or danger of a third, but more often—as here in Gomer's case—the opposite. The required choice, or step, or leap, necessitates a measure of blindfold recklessness and trust. The Osee of the moment is pushed into doing what he thinks, and what

everyone else thinks, is something silly. Pleasurable but silly.
Very well, the more he lives with the result of his act the
more he feels his own part in the original choice, and so
much the more does he put it all down to his own selfishness
and passion. God hides the fact that He has planned the
thing all along. The memory of the soul is short. The Osee of
the moment regrets, repents, looks wistfully at what he might
have done, and very nearly gives up hope. 'Take thee a wife
of fornications,' and the stronger the soul that is called upon
to 'take the wife,' so much the clearer does it see how very
full of fornications that wife is. The eyes of the weaker are
allowed to open gradually; God does not shock us all at once
with the frailties of human nature in case we should shrink
from pledging ourselves to its service.

'And have of her children of fornication.' The life that
God has put them in is not the life they see themselves 'cut
out' to lead. A life against their post-conceptions of themselves. Not only to the chosen ones does this apply—the Osees
that walk in the secret ways of God—but also in a measure
does the law affect us all. God places us somewhere on this
amazing world, and, like stranded tourists, we have to find
our way back to Him: not by *any* route, nor by the safest or
most suitable route, but by just that one and no other that
God would have us travel. 'Make thy way known to me
wherein I should walk' we ask in the Psalm, and add 'thy
spirit will lead me to the right land.'[2] In whatever unforeseen
way the spirit leads, that way, we must depend upon it,
will be the only 'suitable' and 'safe' way for us.

Osee, going about his melancholy task of telling people
things which they had no wish to know, would have felt that
hopeless sense of waste, and the utter and unnecessary folly

[2] Ps. cxlii, 8, 10.

of it all; far more galling, this, than the scorn that came to him from others. He had his share of shame indeed ('the prophet is foolish,' said his friends, 'the spiritual man is mad'[3]), but reproaches from outside are as nothing when compared with the feeling that perhaps after all one has been wrong from the beginning. Let it be said before resuming the prophet's mournful tale that, for those whom the Lord is treating as He treated Osee, the day will dawn when the old initial folly will be seen as the herald of countless graces, nay more, as the very means itself of introducing the soul to its real vocation. If blunder it was to have married Gomer years ago it was a blunder provided for, a blunder precipitated and sacramentalized by God, a blunder without which the life of the soul would never have been complete, a blunder calculated to refine, to humble, and to waken trust.

The Gomers of this world are a blessing not a curse, and like all the greater gifts of God, they either make their Osees saints or make them hard. Have no fear, you Osees: only by missing your own vocations could you have stumbled upon the vocation of God. Can you not remember how all these things began? . . . 'And the LORD said: Go, take thee a wife . . . ' See, surely it has been the work of God.

iii

When Osee took Gomer to wife he probably thought that the Lord's sole purpose was to rescue the woman by linking her to one who, by profession at least, stood for the things of God as opposed to the things of the world. Yes, that was it, Gomer's welfare and not his own, was aimed at by the Lord. . . . Ah well, so long as God was pleased. . . . 'And she conceived and bore a son.'

[3] ix, 7.

Osee was not even allowed to name the boy, so closely did the Lord control that house; 'Jezrahel,' 'The Scattering of God,' was what the eldest son was called, and in giving this frightful name to the first of Osee's seed the Lord seems to hint that the children will take after their mother. Another child; a little girl this time, and for her is the ominous name —God-given again—of 'Without Mercy.' A third. And with every new baby a new fear would have to be faced in the name that the child would have to bear. 'And he [the Lord] said: Call his name: Not My People, for you are not my people. . . . ' A terrible thing to hear on the day of your son's christening! Even while she bore him children it seems that the woman was wanton, 'for their mother hath committed fornication,' says Osee, 'she that conceived them is covered with shame, for she hath said: I will go after my lovers that give me my bread and my water, my wool and my flax, my oil and my drink.' Not satisfied with that, she left him altogether.

We have no idea as to when in Osee's life this crisis came about; nor do we know how old his children were at the time, but it seems fairly clear that Osee, poor man, the constant recipient of messages from God and trembling with an unspoken word within him, was busied with having to bring up a family by himself. And what a family—with names like theirs, and already poisoned by their mother's shame. Osee appears to have been fired at first with a sort of hatred for the woman he had loved and tried to save, and one scarcely wonders at it. We read of him determining to 'lay open her folly in the eyes of her lovers, and no man shall deliver her out of my hand.' But then, when he realizes the depths to which she has fallen, his heart softens and the old longing to draw the still beautiful creature out of the mud overcomes his bitterness and he decides to throw away his plan of exposing her. Instead he will win his wife all over again. 'Behold,' says Osee, and can there be a more generous resolve than this outside the promises we hear from Christ? 'Behold, I will allure her, and will lead her into the wilderness, and I will speak to her heart.'

Though he would win her, this time it would be a wooing with a difference. Instead of the prompt passionate embrace of before, there would now be years when the two would but meet at arm's length: 'Thou shalt wait for me many days, thou shalt not play the harlot . . . and I also shall wait for thee.' The time of segregation would be bitter enough, God knew, almost as hard to bear as the time of loneliness, yet they would not stay apart for ever; 'she shall call me: my husband,' says the prophet with a wonderful confidence; there would be a new home built up of a new and mutual understanding. But these were days as yet far off, the immediate problem was to get her back.

Nothing was wanting to Osee's cup of bitterness, the man had to *buy* her back. The lover who had had her and had tired of her was not ashamed to receive of Osee the price of a slave; 'I bought her to me' is the husband's grim statement of the incident, 'for fifteen pieces of silver and for half a core of barley.' That done, Gomer was safe enough at last, and from what we can see she made the most of her redemption. She was a woman who must have wrecked the lives of many in her time, and it was no fault of hers that Osee's was not one of them, but at the end at least she seems to have known the joys of repentance.

So that is the story of Osee and Gomer. Love, disgrace, penance and probably (no more can be said than that—probably) even conjugal restoration. And all the while the husband is a prophet of the Lord. What memories he must have had to haunt him; those early days with Gomer, for instance, those slightly later days with the children, before they had shown signs of evil promise . . . and all the time he was leading that prophet life of prayer and preaching, of listening to the word of God and writing it. He had his countrymen to grieve over and—with little enough to go upon himself—to rouse in them the grace of hope. Even if Gomer's amendment had never come about in fact, the prophet's tortured yet tremendous faith is voiced in the cry which proclaims, before ever he set himself to regain her, that 'she shall sing there according to the days of her coming up out of the land of Egypt.' This is not the language of a withered man. Broken he may have been but still was he wonderfully alive.

iv

Short though it is, the record of Osee's domestic life is bristling with minor difficulties. The whole account occupies no more than forty verses of Scripture, two-thirds of which are the words of the Lord addressed to Israel, and it is not always easy to tell where the Lord begins and where Osee ends.[4] But if pardon is to be the distinctive note of Osee's gospel, we like to think, not only of God forgiving Israel, not only of Osee forgiving Gomer, but of Gomer's profiting in fact by her husband's promised absolution. True, all that was required for Osee's spiritual development was the attitude of heart—he could have learned the virtue of mercy without ever having had to apply it—but for the consummation of the act of pardoning the welcome of the woman home seems

[4] Indeed for my part I am not by any means certain that I have sifted the text correctly. Those who have it that Gomer was never admitted to her former place as wife would argue that the texts referred to above are applicable only to the Lord's invitations and guarantees to Israel.

necessary. In effect we like to think—and surely from the
text we may legitimately think—of the prematurely aged
prophet, hot-blooded still in spite of his asceticism, leading
back his bride to the desolate home of their early married
life. We think of the mixed feelings that would have torn at
the heart of the prophet as he rose on that eventful day. Almost before it is light he is about the house, sweeping it
himself, and with his own hands preparing a dish that will
keep until the evening—a salad of sorts, richer than what he
is accustomed to and spiced with Gomer's favourite herbs.
We see him on his knees in prayer with the early morning sun
streaming down upon the boards that he has scrubbed the
day before; we see him as he sets out for the market-place of
whatever neighbouring town it is that has advertised the
sale of slaves; he is fasting still and wearing the shirt of hair
beneath his tunic; we hear him jingling in his pocket the
price that will pay for a slave. There is the noise of the
auction . . . how shamefully do these bidding cries strike on
the ears of Osee as he draws near to the place of human mart.
Imagine the coarse jokes . . . the undisguised scrutinies . . .
the judgements passed on muscle, looks, and age . . . the touts
. . . the non-bidders who come from idle curiosity alone. . . .
Oh, horrible to the man of God. We can picture the slight stir
that Osee's presence causes, followed by the silence as his
hand is raised to help the creature from the platform on
which the slaves are ranged. There is the contrast between
her clothes and his (for Osee would not have attempted to
dissemble his profession by dressing to suit the occasion); not
that the prophet was elegant in what he wore, it was the
shabby finery of her costume that made men smile as they
compared the two. Gomer had made no secret of her kind.
As we turn to leave the scene in the company of husband and

wife, we can just see over our shoulder the nudging, pointing crowd, and hear the voices of Osee's sarcastically congratulating acquaintances. Insinuating observations are dropped by passers-by: 'Familiar indeed is Osee with the scandals of the race' . . . 'Chastity begins at home' . . . 'So the clay is common after all, king and commoner, prophet and profligate' . . . and the rest.

Then the journey back. Is it too fanciful to picture Osee after a tiring day of embarrassing encounters, making towards his unpretentious doorway with his wife's hand in his and with the evening sun throwing their gaunt shadows before them on the path? Few words have passed between them since they left the market-square together, and there is silence now as the two step over the threshold. She knows the house of course, every inch of it, and is quick to read his meaning as he leads her gently past his room, *their* room, to what will be her own. 'Thou shalt wait for me many days . . . and I also shall wait for thee.'

Can we not almost see the husband's face, flushed but drawn, as the hand which has held the woman's drops to his side and he backs against the wall to let her pass? That room is hers in which to build up anew the ruins of her life, and he must 'wait' outside. Once in his own quarters Osee sinks to his knees and prays. Surely it has been a great day; a day of many distractions, it is true, but distractions not wholly unrelated to the Lord. A day of unfathomable emotions: a day which must have ended in unfathomable peace.

v

The remaining fourteen chapters are of a vastly different interest; they comprise, as has been suggested, the burden of the prophet's diatribe. Here, though the writing lacks polish and the arrangement is haphazard, we find an unmistakable theme running through all the wealth of metaphor and historical allusion. Even if not the result of deliberate skill, the refrain of sin, penance, mercy . . . sin, penance, mercy . . . but always mercy drowning and crowning all, is impressive and significant. Osee weighs up the corruption of Israel and beats his menacing gong, but it is not with the rampaging harshness of one who regards himself as an alien, aloof from the manners of his kind. It is much more with the reluctant cry of the fellow-sufferer and fellow-countryman (which he was) urging to penance his own flesh and blood before the inevitable dissolution. The prophecy is throbbing with sympathy rather than with sarcasm, and though invective is freely distributed throughout, we have always the feeling that when glaring abuses are attacked, whether royal, sacerdotal, or popular, it is only to lay bare the root evils from which they spring. As a boy Osee had lived in and about the 'Ephraim' cities, and as a man he was come to proclaim, unwillingly one feels, the overthrow of the people he loved.

Osee never doubted for a moment what his mission involved. It would mean his becoming an outcast in his own land; but had he not been lonely in his own home? It would mean—or so he must have thought—almost certain death at the hands of one or other of the victims of his pen and tongue. It would mean estrangement from his own children, other-minded as they were from him; estrangement, too, from the 'consolations of religion,' since the clerical body was among the foremost of those who earned his reprobation. Osee was cutting himself off, in short, from all that would under happier circumstances have made for a life of peaceful retirement and prayer. From the day that Osee first heard of his dismal mission he got no peace but what was granted to his soul by God direct.

Briefly to touch upon the denunciations which Osee hurls at Israel: the prophet suggests at the outset and in the chapters which we have regarded as being particularly his own that even in Jeroboam's massive sway there could be traced a fatal weakness.[5] His rule was 'without mercy' and so, like the metallic figure in Nabuchodonosor's dream, was fated to collapse. (Osee would have rejoiced to read in Daniel's later page that though 'iron breaketh into pieces and subdueth all things,' the kingdom that 'shall take its origin from iron' can hardly stand.[6])

From the veiled hint Osee proceeds to the accusation direct and censures first the flock and then the pastors. 'Like people,' he thunders, having had his say about the layman's morals, 'like priests,' and goes on to expose the deplorable state of the clergy. 'With their flocks and their herds,' says the prophet, 'they shall go to seek the Lord and shall not find him, he is withdrawn from them.' From the money-mindedness which he detects in the very temple itself, Osee turns again to the throne, and sinister allusions are made to what has been going on, reign after reign (and they were brief enough just then) behind the palace walls. The final group of maledictions—if any idea of 'grouping' is possible where no conscious framework seems to have been attempted—would appear, from the infamies it deals with and the mention it makes of the Assyrian menace, to have been written not very long before the fall, and therefore in King Osee's reign. Hope is still held out to the wayward vacillating people of Israel and Osee's

[5] Personal as these passages are there does seem to be a connection between the names of Osee's children and the political situation in Israel at the time of their birth. See Farrar, *Minor Prophets*, p. 76.
[6] Dan. ii. 40, 41.

prophecy ends, as we have just seen, under the ominous-looking clouds of foreign invasion; clouds which could as well be blown away by penance as pricked by continued defiance. Whether Osee died before or after Samaria's fall (c. 720 B.C) we do not know.[7] Neither do we know whether Gomer was with him when he came to write the concluding verses of his book. It is to be hoped, on the whole, not. We prefer to think of that colossal act of faith—'for the ways of the Lord are right, etc.'—as blindly heralding her coming back rather than as the wide-eyed messenger of thanks.[8]

It is not easy to sum up the Book of Osee in a word because so unsystematic is that author's method that he forgets to sum it up himself. Posterity has perhaps been wisely guided in selecting the particular verse it has selected, since of all the trenchant phrases found in Osee, almost the only one to be connected with his name to-day is that to which Our Lord Himself referred: 'I desired mercy and not sacrifice . . . the knowledge of God more than holocausts.' Here we have the prophet's scorn for the empty ritualism which was all around him, the sham penance, the culpable ignorance of the things of God. Here we have also the ever-insistent underlining of God's Love . . . 'I desire Mercy' is the burden of the prophet Osee. Vain is your sacrifice, he seems to say, vain your reforms, your vows, your priesthood even, vain, vain, vain. Come, let us look beneath the skin of things—'knowledge,' supernatural knowledge, rather than 'sacrifice,' superficial sacrifice—come, let us look at Truth Itself . . . come, let us buy back

[7] Fr. Hugh Pope thinks he lived to see it, and quotes iii, 4; vii, 3, 5; viii, 10; x, 3, 7; etc.

[8] This would only mean that the last chapter was finished before the events recorded in the third were rounded off. There is nothing to show that Osee, with Gomer at his elbow and wishing to tell the world how grateful he was to God, did not complete the detached and private section of his prophecy later on.

again with hot repentant tears the place we held before that
throne of Truth. . . . Come. . . .

The case is the same with Osee as with the other prophets:
that where the doom is heaviest, the promises that follow are
the most generous. Osee is at once the Doctor of Love and the
Prophet of the Cross: sin to be blotted out by pain, and pain
to be taken up with love. Punishment, says Osee in effect,
is never meant to crush but to refine. God's tenderness is
every bit as real as is His wrath. Our sufferings are measured
by the largeness of our hearts. If human love—as Osee if
anyone had reason to appreciate—was able in the face of infidelity to stand, then Love Divine, however injured, could
equally survive.

We feel when we come to the end of his book that Osee
is spent with many cursings but that he has spared his failing
breath that he may bless. 'I shall be as the dew,' he says,
speaking in the person of the Lord, 'Israel shall spring as the
lily . . . I will hear him and I will make him flourish like the
green fir-tree. . . . ' There is no cursing here, no anger, no
reproach, but only love.

II. *Joel: The Shadow*

i

IF THERE is little to go upon in the weaving of a 'life' about the prophet Osee, there is very much less in the case of Joel. There is but one single verse, and that only tells us that he was 'the son of Phatuel.' Whatever else there is that can be gleaned about the man must be squeezed out of his three-chaptered prophecy, and so reticent is its almost spectral author that there is uncommonly little to show when all is said. This is one reason why we have ventured to call Joel the 'shadow'; another is because he appears to be the 'shadow' of several other and more substantial prophets who went before him.

At the head of each of the Books of the New and Old Testament (Douay Version as annotated by Challoner) there is a little paragraph in small print to introduce the text. These forewords are a great help in getting a general idea of the setting, but since they lay no claim to infallibility we can say without fear of hurting consciences that the little paragraph at the head of Joel's Prophecy is probably incorrect. It tells us that Joel and Osee were more or less contemporaries—Osee preaching in Israel, Joel in Judea. There is nothing to prove that this was not the case but as far as one can see, and subject always to anything that the Church may have to say about it, it would rather seem that Joel's dates were later. Only the boldest critic would dare to assign even a margin of years, and far be it from the nature of this sketch to juggle with figures when it is well known that the experts on this prophecy differ from one another to the extent of four centuries, yet it certainly does seem—if the much-used argument from silence can be made to prove anything at all—that a clean sweep had taken place of the abuses mentioned by Osee and Amos before the prophet Joel came to write his carefully modelled, but apparently quite unlocatable appeal.

Since, then, there is no 'human story' attaching to this prophet, his somewhat inhuman prophecy can claim our attention straight away.

I call the prophecy of Joel 'inhuman,' not because it is unfeeling or ruthless, or in any way even hard in tone (for it is quite the contrary), but because, being impersonal, it is apt to ring on a colder note than do the less abstract hymns of his fellow-prophets. Where others have had a particular message for a particular people, applicable only at a particular period in history, Joel throws out what is a cross between a dirge and a canticle—call it a song—which is at once cosmic and timeless. It is almost as if the prophet deliberately, with other people's prophecies all round him, sat down to write about the familiar subjects of sin, penance and pardon, but to write about them in such a way as to defy his subsequent critics. Joel embodies in his slender prophecy much of what is best in Isaias, Ezechiel, Amos, Sophonias and Micheas, without ever committing himself to these prophets' specific recriminations. As a fact, of course, there must have been some quite definite provocation—though it is impossible historically to trace it—which resulted in Joel's 'blow ye the trumpet in Sion, sound an alarm in my holy mountain . . . because the day of the Lord cometh,' but actually what he has to say is as applicable to the twentieth century as it is to any one cycle of Jewish history. Joel seems, accordingly, to be the most present-day of all the Minor Prophets. Further, his words can be bent to meet the ups and downs of individual souls as well as the ups and downs of nations, and since souls are always the same however much nations change, Joel is worthy of a hearing at the side of the most recent Friar Preacher. Certain stages, indeed, of the spiritual life find such exact expression in his words that of all these misty prophetical figures there is perhaps none who can hold out so solid a hand to the light-starved soul of any and every age. One might go even further and say that with the possible exception of the psalms there are few passages in the whole of the Old Testament that are capable of giving such consolation as are those to be found in the second chapter of Joel's book.

One feels about this dim and distant prophet as one feels about S. John of the Cross: that after reading him he is not dim and distant in the least; and not only that the more he is read the more he is understood, but that the more he is read the more is he seen to have himself experienced every word of what he writes. To probe deeply it is necessary to have felt *as* deeply, and both these writers, Joel and John, though they exclude all mention of themselves in what they write (unlike, for example, Osee in the category of prophet and Teresa in the category of saint), are only so sure and so searching by reason of what their souls have undergone.

ii

As regards Joel's style and method there is something in the very way in which the prophet opens—especially coming as it does in our Version immediately after the untamed broken strophes of Osee—which is almost twentieth-century in feeling. 'Hear this, ye old men,' says Joel, 'and give ear, all ye inhabitants of the land; did this ever happen in your days

or in the days of your fathers?' It is as arresting as a headline.
It is a sad enough state of affairs that Joel goes on to deplore,
but he is never for a moment dreary in the deploring of it;
his is a cry of pain, it is true, but the wound that is suffered
need not be unto death. 'Gird yourselves and lament, O ye
priests; howl, ye ministers of the altars; go in, lie in sackcloth,
ye ministers of my God; because sacrifice and libation is cut
off from the house of your God . . . to thee, O Lord, will I
cry . . . yea, and the beasts of the field have looked up to thee
as a garden bed that thirsteth after rain.' Mourn, yes, but call
upon the Lord . . . do penance by all means, but as an expectant dog you must look up . . . as a thirsty plant you must
look *up*. 'To thee have I lifted up my eyes who dwellest in
the heavens . . . have mercy on us, O Lord, have mercy on
us.'[1]

We might notice here the stress that is laid in Joel upon
the value of a fast. Even Jeremias, who if anyone, we would
have thought, must have inculcated the necessity of that form
of penance, is less emphatic than Joel. Of the other prophets
that preceded him Isaias and Zacharias are the only two to
mention the practice, and then in weaker terms than he does.
Judith 'fasted all the days of her life except the sabbaths and
new moons and the feasts of the house of Israel,'[2] while Esther
and Daniel were almost equally strict with themselves,[3] but
these are instances of personal ascetic practices, not injunctions to a line of conduct. It is true that we get Jonas and
Esdras insisting on a fast, but even these, together with those
just quoted, are names that belong to post-dispersion and
Machabean times.[4] The question of fasting is a popular or
unpopular theme for the spiritual writer according to whether

[1] Ps. cxxii.   [2] Judith viii, 6.   [3] Esther ix, 31; Dan. ix, 3.
[4] Jonas iii, 5; 1 Esdras viii, 21; see Farrar, op. cit., p. 110.

he is caught in the wave for penance or is forced to stand and brave the same waters on the rebound. At the present, fasting —for the sake of the soul's health—is not considered either wise or necessary. It is thought safer to pray instead. And found easier. There will be a return, it is to be hoped, to the doctrine of the prophets—which is also the doctrine of Christ ('when the bridegroom shall be taken away from them, then shall they fast'), and in those days we may expect to see some answer to those prayers we are so ready to make *without* fasting. Are we, who are clever enough to detect morbidity in penance without prayer, *as* clever in detecting a mere culture in prayer without penance? The prophets fasted; the Apostles fasted; the saints of every period in the Church's history fasted; the people who listen to the word of God to-day, and get things done for Him, are fasting hard . . . and who are we to hold aloof? 'I am not able' if you like, but not, a hundred thousand times not, 'I do not think it necessary.' We have only to read the revelations made by Our Lord to such mystics as S. Margaret of Cortona, Blessed Anna Maria Taigi, Blessed Henry Suso, Mother Frances of the Mother of God, and a whole host of others, to realize what Christ thinks of fasting and of the reasons we give that excuse.

Joel, then, probably knew—as Daniel certainly knew—that where the particular inconvenience of fasting was absent, the other inconveniences of the penitential life would hardly flourish. And is it not always so? Austerity in general is salted by abstinence in particular, and 'austerity in general' is a very important part in the turning of the man towards its Lord. True, it is not the most important part because man is made of soul and body, and the soul must reach out towards God by prayer before ever the body is subdued by punishment . . . but punishment is needed all the same, precisely for that very reason—because man *is* body and soul. When S. John B. Vianney was told that everything had been tried to obtain a favour—prayer, pilgrimages, votive candles, etc., 'Tried blood?' was the Curé's question. The saints, at all events, found that blood flowed more freely for a little fasting.

To return to Joel, there is nothing gloomy about that prophet for all his talk of darkness, as there is nothing acid for all his emphasis on reparation. His eyes may be wet with weeping but they are 'always on the Lord' . . . 'for he is gracious and merciful, patient and rich in mercy . . . who knoweth but he will return . . . and forgive . . . and leave a blessing behind him?' The great whirlwinds that blow through Joel's pages are bracing as well as blasting. He stands, one might say, on the top of a mountain—a volcanic mountain—with one hand holding a trumpet to his lips and pointing with the other to the heavens. He is calling upon a poor wretched dark-nighted flock below in the valley, calling upon them to mourn but not to mope, calling them to come up and sit no more among the ruins of their lives . . . faded lives . . . discouraged lives . . . 'blow ye a trumpet in Sion, sanctify a fast, call ye a solemn assembly . . . between the porch and the altar the priests, the Lord's ministers, shall weep and shall say: Spare, O Lord, spare thy people! . . . ' How grand it is! And again, 'Let them come, let all the men of war come up. Cut your plough-shares into swords and your spades into spears. Let the weak say: I am strong . . . ' Confidence, always confidence, and see how the Lord rejoices in this trust: '. . . and the Lord answered and said to his people: Behold I will send you corn and wine and oil, and you shall be filled with them; and I will no more make you a reproach among the nations.' No sooner, then, has Sion shown her trust than all her years of dryness, plague, and doubt are amply and perfectly made good: ' . . . and I will restore to you the years which the locust and the bruchus and the mildew and the palmer-worm have eaten . . . and you shall eat in plenty and shall be filled . . . and you shall praise the name of the Lord . . . and'—O blessed word for those whose agony has led them nigh to doubt—'you shall *know* that I am in the midst of Israel . . . I am the Lord your God and there is none besides . . . and my people shall not be confounded for ever.' All this does the trusting Joel prophesy, all this is in the power of God to grant; in Osee we have had the God who loves and who is lovable in return, in Joel we have God the Merciful, the God who comes to the rescue with His 'light,' His 'sweetness' and His 'milk' . . . with which Judea's hills shall flow.

'Only hold on a little longer,' Joel seems to say, 'only show to the Lord that you can rise above your sorrow and work the works of God in spite of lassitude within and plague without, and He will "gather you together" and you shall *know* that He is the Lord your God.' (Twice in this short three-chaptered book does this promise of an all-replacing knowledge come—know *that* and you need never fear again.) 'And *so,*' continues Joel, 'put ye in the sickles for the harvest is ripe, come . . . for the press is full, the vats run over . . . and the Lord shall roar out of Sion and utter his voice out of Jerusalem; and the heavens and the earth shall be moved, and the Lord shall be the hope of his people, and the strength of the children of Israel, and you shall *know* that I am the Lord your God dwelling in Sion my holy mountain; and Jerusalem shall be holy and strangers shall pass through it no more. And it shall come to pass in that day, that mountains shall drop down sweetness, and the hills shall flow with milk, and waters shall flow through all the rivers of Juda; and a fountain shall come forth of the house of the Lord, and shall water the torrent of thorns.' Is there a promise richer than this in the whole of Sacred Scripture? No, for it is the promise of a Saviour. Fountains of grace . . . rivers of peace . . . milk and oil and wine in the place of thorns. . . .

How Pauline it all is! '. . . forgetting the things that are behind and stretching forth myself to those that are before, I press towards the mark . . .'[5] 'Be renewed in the spirit of your mind, and put on the new man . . . rise, thou that sleepest, and arise from the dead; and Christ shall enlighten thee . . . see therefore, brethren, how you walk . . . redeeming the time, because the days are evil.'[6] '. . . accounting that God is able to raise up even from the dead . . .'[7] and, lastly, that classic exhortation to 'persevere under discipline; God dealeth with you as with his sons . . . all chastisement for the present indeed seemeth not to bring with it joy but sorrow; but afterwards it will yield, to them that are exercised by it, the most peaceable fruit of justice. . . . Wherefore lift up the hands which hang down and the feeble knees . . . and make straight steps with your feet . . .'[8] Yes, we shall have to fight for it; both of them, prophet of God and preacher of Christ, they both say that we shall have to pay the price of faith and hope, but the result, as Joel says in the words with which he closes his book—words we should by now have expected him to use, so constantly does he revert to this idea—is that our hope is justified, for 'the Lord will dwell in Sion.' And that is all. It has been worth it, says the tired but trusting soul. For a moment the cloud has been pierced, and in the shaft of light was written GOD.

---

[5] Phil. iii, 13.
[6] Eph. iv, 23-4; 14, 15, 16.
[7] Heb. xi, 19.
[8] Heb. xii, 7, 11, 12.

iii

It has been said above that there is reason to believe that some sort of cleaning up had taken place in Israel, both in the Northern and Southern Kingdoms, between the time of the Osee-Amos mission and the time of Joel's appearance. In Joel's prophecy there is the same insistence upon the need for a return to the way of the Lord as there is in the other two prophets, but nowhere does Joel urge the same reasons for its necessity. The kings, it appears, had not been misbehaving themselves—at all events he never mentions them; the priests, though urged in no uncertain terms to do penance, are nowhere spoken of as having deserved, by any specifically evil practices, the penance which they are expected to undertake. Idolatry is not referred to and the drunkenness and immorality, which are ever found to loom so large on the horizon of other prophets, are barely mentioned here. The thing that seems particularly to distress the prophet Joel is not this and that abuse, so much as the evil consequences of sin that have resulted in the twofold disaster of the country's decline on the one hand and the 'cutting off' of the Lord's sacrifice and libation on the other. *That* is why satisfaction must be made, *that* is why the priests—responsible for the flock, though not responsible for the sin—are to howl and lie in sackcloth, and to fast and call out: 'Spare.' In fact, one can almost trace here a suggestion of sympathy and respect in his mention of the clergy. So much so that it is claimed that Joel was himself a priest.

He is hard on no class of society, and only directly inveighs against the unbeliever; he is hard on *him*—very hard—for the trade he has made of Jewish prisoners. Joel is free of allusions to foreign politics, and is silent also about the activities of the Northern Kingdom, thus beyond his vague but unmistakable references to a recent captivity there is nothing in the prophecy to show that Joel was not simply talking in the air about the need to prepare for the judgement which was to precede the ultimate deliverance of Juda.

It is no part of a rough sketch such as this is to worry out allusions in the text that have baffled the critics of at least three European nations. Accordingly I spare discussion as to whether or not the plague of locusts which occupies the best part of Joel's second chapter is meant to be taken literally; nor need we wonder to what particular invasion it refers, if the account is nothing but a symbol; the most that we need volunteer is that, if symbol it is, the passage lacks nothing of vividness and life. Here again, in the choice of his similes as well as in the perfection of his periods, Joel reminds us forcibly of that which is most virile in the literature of to-day. 'A numerous and strong people, as the morning spread upon the mountains'; he refers repeatedly to the mountains; like S. John of the Cross and his Carmel, Joel finds much to satisfy him in the imagery of the heights: 'before the face thereof a devouring fire and behind it a burning flame; the land is like a garden of pleasure before it, and behind it a desolate wilderness; neither is there anyone that can escape it . . . the appearance of them [the locusts] is as the appearance of horses, and they shall run like horsemen. They shall leap like the noise of chariots upon the tops of the mountains, like the noise of a flame of fire devouring the stubble . . . at their presence the people shall be in grievous pains, all faces shall be made like a kettle'—a kettle, if you please!—'. . . they shall fall through the windows and shall take no harm; they shall enter the city; they shall run upon the wall; they shall climb up the houses; they shall come in at the windows as a thief . . . Now, therefore, be converted, etc.' And then, following upon the call to repentance, comes the consoling news of what is to be the reward of the change of heart: the Lord will pour out his spirit upon all flesh, the young shall see visions and shall prophesy, and the ancients, enjoying their prerogative, shall spend their last days dreaming dreams. Finally, shall the Lord 'judge all nations round about,' and when that is done, the children of the Lord will live happily ever after.

iv

And so Joel, wrapping his silver trumpet in the parchments of other men's prophecies, comes down from his beloved mountain and is swallowed up once more in the mists of the valley. The notes that the old man has sounded will be tossed from peak to peak as long as the world survives. We think of him as a dreamy priest, too much lost in the clouds to grapple with problems of morality, and perhaps even too tired with fasting to want to; ideals rather than abuses are the concern of Joel; for him it is to stir in the hearts of men (what I believe is called) an 'efficacious hope.' Joel is—to use that much-wasted word—the mystic. Expression fails him in which to clothe his ecstasy, and the phrases of Isaias, Ezechiel, Amos and Micheas have to serve. Joel is none the less great for that, none the less mystic, none the less searching, but only on the face of it less strikingly original; and, after all, once granted Inspiration, does it very much matter if quills that were used before are dipped in the ink again?

After this it will indeed be interesting to find when we get to heaven that an unassuming, absent-minded little prophet —a priest, and introduced to us as 'son of Phatuel'—is the centre of an admiring group that is noting every word of what he says. 'They turn to him,' we may be told, 'for everything . . . do Amos, Isaias, Ezechiel and Micheas.'

III. *Amos: The Poet-Socialist*

i

THE destiny of prophets is proverbial. Earnest readers for whom generalizations must be verified might well be given the name of Amos to head the list of those who vindicate the sorry boast. If any prophet was the victim of intrigue and persecution it was this one; the story of Amos is as dramatic as that of Osee, with the additional romantic detail that the hero is a shepherd-boy . . . and one who can master words. An account of Amos' career might fittingly reach the world from the pages of Grimm or Andersen; tucked away in the folds of Juda's hills, bronzed by exposure and lithe of limb, the youthful herdsman is provided with a task; he does it; he returns; it is only the fortune at the end of it that is lacking in the prophet's case.

'The words of Amos who was among the herdsmen of Thecua'—the prophecy begins—'which he saw concerning Israel in the days of Ozias king of Juda, and in the days of Jeroboam the son of Joas king of Israel, two years before the earthquake.' Thecua appears to have been an obscure village in the Southern Kingdom, and it was from here that Amos could watch the growing worldliness of those who came over the border from the North. There were wicked men and rich in his own native Juda, but the nobles of Israel who would ride over his quiet meadows and trample down his father's corn, surpassed anything he met with at home. What was going on in Juda, either from the point of view of church or

state, need not concern us since the whole of Amos' prophetical life was cast in Israel. The Jeroboam whom the prophet
mentions as ruling in the North is the same Jeroboam the
Second who fixes the date of Osee for us, only this time we
shall come upon him earlier in the reign; it was he, as we
have seen, who had gained for Israel much of that nation's
prosperity, and it was to him therefore that Amos, following
his flocks from afar, attributed the blame for what he saw.
Amos longed as earnestly as any devout believer that the two
nations should be united, but he feared that his own less pro-
gressive Juda would be infected by her disorderly sister over
the way; he prayed to the Lord for a solution; a part at least
of his prayer was answered when it was appointed that his
own rude herdsman's voice should be raised in the threatening of nations and the condemning of kings.

Looking at the text we see that the prophet plunges straight
away into what the Lord has bidden him tell to Israel, and it
is not until his message is two-thirds through that Amos
draws breath to tell us something of himself. Following his
example, we shall treat first of his 'burden' and then of the
book's narrative element—the way in which that burden was
received.

ii

It must be borne in mind that what Amos said to Israel
was not said in the way that Osee, for example, was to say
it—or something very much like it—a few years later in the
reign; Amos spoke as a stranger. There are several points of
resemblance between the two prophets, but one of the main
differences between them is that where Osee, as a native and
a patriot, saw deep down into the country's rottenness—and
saw with sympathy—Amos, on the other hand, saw merely

that things were wrong. He was to denounce the nation for many things, but his first consideration was to show that the high standard of living was running away with the country's moral sense and the duties which it owed to God. Amos knew where to lay the blame and how to lay it; his congenital anti-aristocratic bias saw to it that he did so. This is why the prophet was so hardly used. There is a sting in his address that Osee lacks; it is certainly significant that where prompt and violent measures are taken to silence Amos, the more dangerous prophet Osee—more specific, too, in his condemnations—is suffered to walk at large.

Amos directs his first attack against idolatry; in the case of his own Juda, he says, it is 'their idols that have caused them to err,' and he sees in Israel's infidelity the same germ at work. In three distinct sermons, each beginning with the same words, Amos outlines the fate of the apostate nation.[1] In five equally well-defined visions[2] the prophet warns the whole people of Israel, passes sentence, and then finally promises release to a remnant; his prophecy ends as hopefully as any other.

Now Israel was not accustomed to these visionaries; the only prophets it had known for some time had been those of the Jonas pattern, laying down no very stern doctrine at home whatever they might do in the way of preaching penance abroad. And here was a wild-looking person of the old school, Amos the Southerner, a man of God if ever there was one, a distant echo of Elias himself (already almost a legend) . . .

---

[1] ix, 11, 15. Fr. Pope draws attention to the fact that Ch. iv (though our version does not bring it out) is a special indictment, against women. This throws a new light on our fierce young apostle.

[2] To do with locusts, fire, the plastering of a wall, the gathering of fruit, the judgment of the Lord as He stands upon the altar; the visions could hardly have been more various in subject-matter.

and come to tell the chosen people how to behave. In a civilized age it was not to be endured. Samaria might sit through a spirited harangue once in a way and enjoy it, especially if it came from a fashionable preacher, but when her faults were pointed out by self-established messengers of God—and this one a farm-hand from Juda—the thing was an outrage. In part we can understand the objection: Amos was not a priest; he was not a certified scribe; he was not even a student of the Law; *and* he was not a gentleman. Amos did not have a chance.

As it happened the farm-hand spoke (if his preaching was like his prose) with singular finish and correctness; he reveals a culture and refinement, the experts tell us, that must have been rare at that time even in the centres of education, let alone on the rugged hill-tops of Judea. Fr. Pope suggests that Amos' connection with the wool trade established for the prophet contacts which would have been closed to the peasant in the ordinary way, and that this might account for the many references to Egypt. A much-travelled Amos, however, makes admittedly no very great appeal, and when we look at the text with the possibility in mind, we are relieved to note that the author of those lyrical strophes had need only to be a penetrating observer of what was going on around his hut. If mystery there is, it is how he came about the art of self-expression; and with Amos the art is at least part-scientific. I quote Farrar for the authority that five words spelt in a curious way are the sole trace of provincialism, and that, even here, the softer pronunciation of the South is possibly attempted.

Even as it stands in the English, the majesty of Amos' style is striking. 'Hear,' he says to the rich, whom he detests (and it is the rich women he particularly has in mind), 'hear this

word, ye fat kine that are in the mountains of Samaria; you
that oppress the needy and crush the poor . . . the Lord hath
sworn by his holiness that, lo, the days shall come upon you
when they shall lift you up on pikes, and what shall remain
of you in boiling pots.' This is the language of oratory, not
perhaps the lofty language that he attains to later on as he
rises to the climax of his message, but a rhetoric it is that has
the unmistakable sweep of the born orator. With all his radical views, Amos is no petty political agitator; the prophet is
indeed out for social reform, a reform of widespread application and prompt execution, but the character of his pro-
gramme is singularly undetailed; it is not so much statistical
as poetical . . . ideal. The peasant does not presume to eco-
nomics—these he leaves to the capitalist (if only that gentleman will do his duty)—the peasant throws out elementary
morality, fundamental principles, and leaves it at that. Or
rather, he returns to it again and again, but always *at that*.
'Seek ye good and not evil' is his precept, 'that you may live,
and the Lord of hosts will be with you' . . . 'hate evil and love
good and establish judgement in the gate; it may be that the
Lord the God of hosts may have mercy . . .' Refusing, then,
to assess in set terms the debit of Israel's infidelity, Amos holds
over Israel's head the inevitable and not far distant consequences; and these consequences, again, the prophet shrinks
from enumerating. 'Woe to them that desire the day of the
Lord; to what end is it for you? The day of the Lord is darkness and not light . . . as if a man should flee from the face
of a lion, and a bear should meet him; or enter into a house
and lean with his hand upon a wall, and a serpent should bite
him . . . shall not the day of the Lord be darkness and not
light, obscurity and no brightness in it? . . . I hate and have
rejected your festivities; I will not receive the odour of your

assemblies . . . ' A curious absence of the precise evils that the Lord shall send upon them, a vague sentence, but none the less certain for its being nameless. '. . . it is as if' is the farthest he will go, and the condemnation is all the more forceful as the result. Amos is enough of a psychologist to know that the sentence will be dreaded most by those who cannot even picture the punishment in store. '. . . Shall not the day of the Lord be darkness and not light, obscurity and no brightness in it?' . . . Amos has studied human nature well. 'Behold, the days come, saith the Lord, and I will send forth a famine in the land; not a famine of bread nor a thirst of water, but of hearing the word of the Lord . . . they shall go about seeking the word of the Lord and shall not find it . . . in that day the fair virgins and the young men shall faint for thirst . . .' It is part of the genius of Amos that he touches the nerves of his hearers as well as their souls; he knows, possibly without even knowing that he knows, how capable a weapon is the secret in the stirring of men's minds, even more capable than the horror.

A word, before we leave the subject of the prophecy and turn to the prophet himself, upon the place of nature in the Book of Amos: of all the prophets, Amos is perhaps the richest in metaphor, and his imagery is for the most part drawn from nature. He refers, like many other poets, to the sunrise; there are frequent allusions to eclipses, to hurricanes, earthquakes, and showers; he knows the names of stars; he speaks of cedars and oaks, of forests and forest fowl; there are glimpses of sheep being rescued from the jaws of lions, birds from snares; there are the homely pictures of men planting vineyards, treading grapes, ploughing, and propping up fallen booths. The canvas of Amos is thick with colour and he lays it on with tremendous energy. Passages as vigorous as this: 'I sent death upon you in the way of Egypt, I slew your young men with the sword even to the captivity of their horses; and I made the stench of your camp to come up into your nostrils; yet you returned not to me, saith the Lord. . . .' and this: 'And after I have done these things to thee, be prepared to meet thy God, O Israel; for behold he that formeth the mountains and createth the wind . . . he that maketh the morning mist and walketh upon the high places of the earth . . . the Lord the God of hosts is his name' . . . such passages follow one another as swiftly as do the flames that he is so fond of . . . that race along the 'walls of Gaza' and devour alike the towns of Bosra, Benadad, Rabbaa and Tyre.

iii

'The Lord will roar from Sion and utter his voice from Jerusalem; and the beautiful places of the shepherds have mourned and the top of Carmel is withered.' These are the first words which Amos spoke in Israel, and if Jerusalem and Carmel are scarcely to be touched upon in the doom that is to follow, they are ominous enough for Israel. But let us go back to Thecua where Amos is still watching his sheep and plucking his wild figs and learning to use his eyes.

Amos would hardly have enjoyed saying good-bye to Thecua, a modest bundle slung across his back. Not that he had far to go—a dozen miles at most—nor, from what we can guess of the fire within him, that the missionary aspect of his task was in any way against the grain. The difficulty would rather come in having to confront a people who were almost of his own race, speaking the same language and probably familiar with his history—what there was of it. If Amos was not afraid of the hardship in store he was probably afraid of the ridicule, and he would have been inhuman had the social question cost him not a thought.

We can picture this rustic youth, then, with burning eyes and tight lips, striding along the sun-baked north-west road that will lead to his wildly imprudent but marvellously purifying vocation. Lizards come out to blink and pant at him, jerking their slippery bodies nervously in the dust; a cloud of flies keeps pace with him, buzzing and swinging to the rhythm of his walk; the sun beats down upon the 'holy land,' and though the country is relieved at times by mud-hut villages and olive groves, by clumps of palms and gardened properties, Amos pays not the slightest heed, he is pondering the message of the Lord. The lizards, aghast at seeing so much resolution, return to their cactus growths to doze, and infinitely patient ants resume their crossing of the north-west road. But allowing that the poet in Amos insisted on occasional attention to the view, even the more broken parts of Ephraim's landscape would have struck him, after the wilderness of Judea, as tamed and over-populated. The breath of the uplands was in the prophet's nostrils as he drew near to the evil-smelling, 'go-getting' cities of Samaria, and one wonders what scornful thoughts were racing through that violently-energizing brain of his, when he exchanged the ritual greeting with those soft-palmed town and suburb dwellers who were to stand for him in the place of his sheep for a time.

Once in Bethel, and having relieved himself of his fearful burden, Amos' story is as follows; we get it from the seventh chapter of his book (and it is as well to note that he gives us more to go upon than anything we have in the other Minor Prophets with the exception of Jonas; and then it is only seven verses of the text).

First of all he was sent for by Amasias the arch-priest of

Bethel. And before we go any further we must take stock, and
at least *aim* at being fair.

Amos, as we have seen, had judged that the deplorable
state of the country was entirely due to the misrule of those in
power—the king, the priests, and the nobly born generally.
He had said so with some feeling. Now the king was too
remote and wonderful a person apparently to have been
affected either way by the denunciation; not sorry, not en-
raged—he may never even have heard of it. The nobles were
too indolent to take any active step, so it fell to the clerical
body to defend the reputation of the whole. Amasias as the
official leader of things ecclesiastical took upon himself the
task of vindication. The day came, then, when the reputable
Amasias, trembling with indignation and bolstered up in his
resolve by the unanimous vote of his chapter, wrote off to the
king suggesting that it was the sovereign's *duty* to prevent
these upstart aliens putting ideas into the heads of his loyal
subjects. 'And Amasias, the priest of Bethel, sent to the king
of Israel, saying: Amos hath rebelled against thee in the midst
of the house of Israel; the land is not able to bear all his
words,' and then the wretched old man quotes some of the
prophet's words, only he quotes them wrong; it is enough to
make one weep. 'For thus saith Amos: Jeroboam shall die by
the sword, and Israel shall be carried away captive out of
their own land.' If Amasias had listened to a sermon from the
prophet's lips he would have known that it was the last thing
Amos would have done—to predict anything so cut and dried.
What Amos *had* said was that the Lord would 'rise up against
the house of Jeroboam with the sword,' and that the mighty
ones of Israel, 'the faction of the luxurious ones,' (not the
whole nation, but only those 'that sleep upon beds of ivory
. . . that eat the lambs out of the flock . . . that drink wine in

bowls and anoint themselves with the best ointments . . .'),
only those shall be 'taken away.' Really it was the limit on the
part of Amasias; misrepresentation of that sort is worse than
a downright lie. Amos could not defend himself here, even if
he would. But it seemed that Amos would not. He was probably expecting as much and looking forward to it. Had he not
said in public: 'You will command the prophets saying:
"Prophesy not" '? and of the prophet on his part, that 'they
have hated him that rebuketh in the gate'?

In an evil generation, men who seek for themselves only
the things of God, and for others what they conceive to be
God's will, must pay the price. Amos' sole regret would have
been that he had not had time to say all that he *could* have
said on the subjects of idolatry and extortion. He would have
known that no man, and least of all an uneducated man, can
go on indefinitely saying things like 'Woe to you that are
wealthy in Sion' without getting into trouble, and Amos *did*
go on saying them. He said: 'Woe to you that have confidence
in the mountain of Samaria.' 'Woe to you,' he added further, far from taking anything back, 'ye great men, heads of
the people, that go with state into the house of Israel.' The
prophet had no more regard for human prudence than he had
for human depravity, and so was not likely to save his skin.
He is only one of the many, sharing his lot with Our Lord
Himself, and, as always when the saint is brought to book,
the charge is made in the name of righteousness and peace.
'Amos hath rebelled against thee . . . the land is not able to
bear his words.' It is as the disturber of the ordered course of
things that Amos is eventually silenced. Attempts to silence
Daniel rested on the same grounds. History is unchanged in
this at least, that it feeds the same kind of people with the
same kind of fare. The expelling Amasias was included in the

soliloquy which we read in Wisdom: 'Let us lie in wait for the just' (say they who have fallen away from grace), 'because he is not of our turn and he is contrary to our doings, and he upbraideth us . . . and divulgeth against us the sins of our way of life . . . he boasteth that he hath the knowledge of God . . . he is grievous to us, even to behold [Amos, uncouth and "of the full field," would hardly have cut a very elegant figure] . . . his life is not like other men's and his ways are very different [this is an invariable charge] . . . let us examine him by outrages and tortures that we may know his meekness and try his patience.'[3] Amos, then, together with Isaias, Jeremias, and Daniel, would have been one of those to whom Our Lord referred when He added to His Beatitude for the Persecuted: 'for so they persecuted the prophets that were before you.'[4] Amos would have been glad to know that part—and surely the major part—of the trial that entitled him to blessedness was to be 'spoken evil of untruly.'

Even now the king seems to have taken no step to suppress the spreader of treasonable doctrine. Jeroboam was probably shrewd enough to read between the lines of Amasias' letter, and judging the matter to be a religious one after all, was either not interested himself, or else suspected that the priest had reason to be too much interested; in effect he left the report unattended to, and Amasias was evidently given to understand that the prophet was his to dispose of as well as might be. Thus when Israel was still smarting from the fierceness of his lash, and when the longing for the solitudes of the hills was upon him, Amos was summoned to an audience with his priest. The meanest imagination can hardly help but reconstruct the scene: Amasias seated in his presbytery hall, with the light behind him that he may watch the face of his

---

[3] Wisd. ii, 11-22.   [4] Matt. v, 11, 12.

visitor; Amos threading his way through the narrow streets, his eyes on the filthy pavement and his thoughts debating as to which were the worst: silly women or rich men. Amasias is ever so slightly apprehensive; Amos not at all. The priest feels that he holds all the cards in his hand but that one never knows with these fanatics, what they will do next. He only hopes there will not be a scene; he hates scenes. There was no need to be nervous; why, the man was almost one's prey (though one would not use the term) and in any case he was vastly one's inferior. One would dismiss the man as one would a domestic . . . ah, here he was . . . well, well, well, one would see.

I cannot imagine Amos except as a tall, rather awkward, sandy-haired young man, with high features and a bold blue eye. The beginnings of a beard tend to soften (and because so tentative, make young) the otherwise sharp outline of a not very intricate cast of face. *So* earnest is his whole address that he is perhaps a little lacking in humour; unconscious, anyway —put it thus—of the incongruous figure he presents . . . in the cool, clean sobriety of the priestly house. There is absolutely no excuse for picturing Amos so; he may have been quite old and a kindly smile may have played about his lips; but I do picture him so, and there it is.

'And Amasias said to Amos: Thou seer, go—flee away to the land of Juda, and eat bread there, and prophesy there. But prophesy not again any more in Bethel because it is the king's sanctuary.' There was no long working up to the final discharge, it was straightforward expulsion in the first sentence; 'go away' was what, bold blue eye or no blue eye, Amos had to listen to. '. . . And it is the house of the kingdom,' adds Amasias, referring to Bethel and breaking, so it seems, the silence that followed. 'And it is the house of the kingdom,' what a remark! There is no reason for making it because he has said as much already, but it shows that he was at a loss; and not knowing what to say, told, for the second time that day, what was oddly enough the truth. The real reason why Amos had to go was simply as he said: God's word was not to be sown on royal land. 'You can't go rampaging about in these parts, my good man, because it is the king's territory.'

Amasias doubtless felt that the interview was at an end; according to schedule the boorish provincial ought to pick up his palm-leaf hat and go. What was he waiting for? Was he as rustic as all that, that he was waiting for leave to depart? well, it was something that he had manners enough to wait. The dumb ox! And glib enough too on the platform, one had heard.

'And Amos answered and said to Amasias: I am not a prophet nor the son of a prophet, but I am a herdsman plucking wild figs'—notice how Amos fastens upon the priest's weakness; to tell Amasias yes, that he *is* a son of the soil, will embarrass the old man if he has any real breeding—'and the Lord took me when I followed the flock, and the Lord said to me: Go, prophesy to my people Israel.' Amos has treated the priest to an autobiographical digression, but only to strengthen the curse he has in store. 'And now hear thou the word of the Lord,' he goes on, and terrible is the charge: 'Thou sayest: thou shalt not prophesy against Israel, and thou shalt not drop thy word upon the house of the idol [Bethel]; therefore thus saith the Lord: Thy wife shall play the harlot in the city, and thy sons and daughters shall fall by the sword, and thy land shall be measured by a line; and thou shalt die in a polluted land, and Israel shall go into captivity out of their land.' Amos commits himself for once; for once Amos comes down from the general to the particular and, if he has been misquoted once, leaves no room for a second misquotation now. It is interesting to note that in the concluding sentence he says what he has not said up to date, but what he had been reported to the king as having said. The speech has a ring about it that, if it sounds challenging enough at this distance, must have sounded very frightening indeed to the person to whom it was addressed. The contempt for the usurped authority is perfectly suggested: here was he, Amos, not a born prophet or 'divinity student' (this is surely what he means when disclaiming the title 'prophet' which Amasias, history, his public—not to say the Church—have applied to him) . . . here was he, plucked away from the hillside almost by the hair of his head—like Habacuc—and planted by the Lord—who else?—in an environment he had no use for. And why? For one reason only, 'to drop God's word.' Amos is perfectly logical and perfectly fair; his reasoning is incontestable. ' . . . So the royal lands may not be littered with the vulgar page of Revelation! Very well, thus and thus will the Lord of hosts perform to those who trifle with, etc., etc.'

. . . .

The palm-leaf hat is picked up; the interview is closed. Amos has closed it. Outside in the open, the prophet stands for a moment and sniffs the tainted air, but the sniffing is that of a horse that scents in prospect the possibility of hay. A yellow wilderness of hair is roughly screened from view, and Amos saws his way back through the busy streets . . . to await inevitable arrest.

As I say, I may be wrong. The real Amos, blinking mischievously at the sun, may have come out into the arcaded court and fanned himself awhile . . . elderly and calm . . .

before taking a turn in the public gardens and so to bed . . .
and nothing to mark him from his fellows but his air of gentle
mirth.

iv

A revelation made by Our Lord to S. Catherine of Siena
runs as follows; the words might as truly have been spoken
to Amos: 'You will have to leave your native town to save
souls. I shall be always with you; I shall lead you out and
bring you back; I shall confide to you the honour of My
Name; and you will teach My doctrine to great and small,
to laymen and to priests and monks. I will give you a speech
and wisdom which no one will be able to resist. I will place
you in the presence of Pontiffs and of the governors of the
Church and of nations, in order to confound by this means,
as I always do, the pride of the powerful.'[5]

Amos, even if he had not 'confounded the powerful' in
his sermons, had most certainly done so in his conversation
with the priest. This particular pontiff nowhere denies the
prophet's mission to preach, he merely denies him the right
of preaching *here;* nor does he question the truth of what is
preached, he merely questions the wisdom of being allowed
to preach it. Therein, surely, lies the horror of the sin; a sin
that is repeated to-day in social and official circles all the
world over: the Gospel and its true apostles are rejected, not
from want of credence, but on grounds of sheer expediency
alone.

To return to S. Catherine and Amos: 'I shall confide to
you,' were Christ's words to the former, 'the honour of My
Name,' and if the preaching in that Name be interrupted,
the preaching in that Name must be resumed. The propheti-

[5] *Life,* by Blessed Raymond, Part II, ch. vi.

cal impulse in Amos had not spent itself in the foretelling of
domestic upheavals to the house of Amasias. Before the
prophet bowed to whatever measures of violence were taken
against him, he delivered himself of a farewell message to
Israel at large, and it is even more menacing than what has
gone before. It is a 'woe' which falls heaviest, as we should
expect, upon 'you that crush the poor, and make the needy
of the land to fail.' (We can compare this with S. Catherine's
'governors of nations' and 'proud powerful.') It is believed
by some that Amos added the final chapter after returning
to the flocks and rocks of Judea, and that this accounts for
the more than usual wealth of hill-imagery.[6] Far be it from
me to enter the discussion; I can only say that I prefer to
think of Amos, once among his sheep again and his lonely
melancholy hills, as bothered no more with the affairs of
men. May we not let him grow old under the purpling sky
of evening and the brazen blaze of day? Must we make him
into a writer, worrying out curses when his blood has cooled,
and dooming from afar those cities where he has preached so
feverishly? No, for Amos it is now the solitude of the heights;
he needs to pray off those corners of his nature; he needs to
be refined, mellowed, humbled even, under the mighty hand
of God . . . and nowhere is that hand so suffered to do its
work as in the chastening school of solitude.

So the story of Amos is the story of Jeremias after him,
and the story of S. Joan and Savonarola later still: unquali-
fied and unretracted preaching followed by arrest; the same
fearless reproving of the very judges responsible for their
seizure . . . and then the silencing. Banned by the clergy,

---

[6] Thus the legend is assumed to be false which brings the prophet home only
to die of wounds when he gets there. The tradition is mentioned in Farrar,
but it does not seem to bear much weight.

condemned by the secular power, and undefended by their public, so these 'seers' of the Lord are wont to die. But their failures do not matter, their subsequent silences and even deaths do not matter; the work they have begun is carried on. Behold in Amos a wild man striding over the hills and in his hand a torch; by the yellow glare of the cities the flame that he carries is smothered . . . but only to furnish embers for the lighting of another brand. Even when Amasias was shrugging his shoulders and turning away from the sight that met him from his windows—the sight of a prophet of God being hounded down the street and out of the city gates —even *then* was there another prophet of God to preach the same doctrine of reform. This new apostle was very likely watching from his balcony what Amasias dared not watch from his; a young man, this, and married only recently, a Northerner, and possibly never heard of by the hermit-shepherd of Thecua. But his is the same spirit, his the same calling, his an even deeper test of hope. For him to tell to Israel of its wedlock with the Lord.

So Amos, very bruised but very happy, is left to himself at last, limping along the road that leads to Juda. He has done his best and there are no regrets . . . and as for what it has cost him, that was the price, perhaps, that 'nature' had to pay . . . perhaps he had worked too selfishly and traded with a zeal a shade too harsh . . . it was only right, so he would tell himself, that his human prejudice should thus be purged. . . .

The sun on his raw skin acts like a blanket; the little stone buildings which he meets occasionally as he drags himself from sleepy village to sleepy village gleam dazzling white among the olive trees and sear his aching eyes; his thoughts go out to a palm-leaf hat . . . it is making relics in Bethel. He is bent, and his feet drag in the dust; he would seem from the distance to be leaning against a quivering wall of heat. The sky—even to this poet—is a blue hot plate pressing him down, and the nervous flicking of grasshoppers adds a further irritant to the tension of the air.

We will not do badly if we follow, ever so distantly, in the footsteps of this saint as he drops wearily over a rise in the ground and is lost to view. Amos is finding—has found—his way home. The fairy-story has ended happily after all.

IV. Abdias: The Sublime

i

THE prophecy of Abdias comes where it does in the Bible because of what Amos has said on the previous page about the desolation of Edom; it is with the pride and fall of that nation that the single chapter of the prophet Abdias is concerned.

The date of the prophecy has never been satisfactorily determined. Catholic opinion seems to put Abdias in the Amos-Osee period—somewhere about the eighth century B.C.; the Jews, who hold this prophet in the greatest reverence on account of their identification of his Edom with Rome, make him very much earlier, while non-Catholic critics for the most part are in favour of assigning a margin of dates between the fall of Jerusalem (c. 587 B.C.) and the Return (c. 537 B.C.).

There is nothing to say about the history of this prophet because nothing whatever is known about him. He gives us no information about himself; he cannot with any degree of certainty be recognized either as Achab's astute steward (3 Kings xviii, 3) or as one of Josaphat's Levite emissaries (2 Par. xviii, 8), and even legend has passed him over. S. Jerome has a word to say about his tomb and the miracles that were wrought at it, but the Abdias of Jerome's Samarian tour is not now, I understand, very generally taken to be the author of the Prophecy. It is from S. Jerome, however, that I have ventured to take the heading which somewhat pretentiously sponsors these tenuous notes. As far as words go, says S. Jerome about Abdias, it is the least of all prophecies, yet in the 'sublimity of its mysteries' it is inferior to none. We take S. Jerome's word for it; he is, we must remember, a Doctor of the Church.

ii

It is not surprising to find that the Israelites have always made much of Abdias, he is almost the only prophet who has no hard word to say of them. He voices moreover one of their dominant sentiments: that they are the only people whom God cares anything about. 'It is for us that thou didst form the earth,' comes in the song of the Purim, 'other nations, O Javeh, are but spittle in thy sight.' Abdias never goes quite as far as that, but his treatment of 'other nations' gives reason to think that he would have liked to.

Edom, the villain-people of the piece, is first of all reproached by Abdias for its smug satisfaction; Edom has become secure, tucked away up there in its rocky honeycomb, and is insular beyond words; 'small among the nations' he calls them, 'exceedingly contemptible' . . . 'the pride of thy heart hath lifted thee up, who dwellest in the clefts of the rocks and settest up thy throne on high; who sayest in thy heart: Who shall bring me down?' This is a telling description of a self-opinionated tribe, cut off from the wider thought of others. There is the Touareg in Africa to-day whose sufficiency is such that the cars and sewing-machines of the French are produced as evidence of that nation's backward civilization in the face of what the camel and the thorn can do. 'Though thou be exalted as an eagle,' is the threat of Abdias, 'and though thou set thy nest among the stars, thence shall I bring thee down, saith the Lord.'

Edom is next reproved for the malicious zest with which it had exulted over Juda's fall. It is a bitter reproach that is hurled at the one-time brother race: 'When strangers carried away his armies captive, and foreigners entered into his gates and cast lots upon Jerusalem, thou also wast one of them. But thou shalt not look on in the day of thy brother, in the day of his leaving his country; and thou shalt not rejoice over the children of Juda in the day of their destruction . . . neither shalt thou stand in the crossways to kill them that flee.' Whenever it was that all this had happened, Edom had evidently behaved very badly; the difficulty is to find out when it did happen. There are several different sackings of the Holy City to which the above might refer. If you take it that the prophecy was written before Nabuchodonosor's invasion you must stretch the 'thou shalt not' to cover a future contingency—and it does not seem likely that Abdias was telling the Edomites what not to do 'in the day of the Lord'—or else you must allow 'thou shalt not' to mean 'it was sin to' and refer the whole passage to one of the previous hostile occupations. Philistines, Arabians, and even Israelites, had swept over the land before the eighth century B.C., so there is nothing to prevent Abdias staying where we put him and writing about one of these defeats. Present-day opinion seems to be, however, that the best way of getting out of it is to make him write his prophecy after the Captivity, referring both lots of censures to that occasion. For our purposes it matters very little. Whether the prophet was thinking of the future or of the past, the sons of Esau had always shown themselves to be a savage crew, revengeful, and ready to 'tread upon their enemy in the gate,' and 'as thou hast done, so shall it be done to thee; he [the Lord] will return thy reward upon thy own head.' One wonders how many people ever

connect the name of Abdias with anything so nearly approaching to what was happily twisted by Our Lord into the Golden
Rule.

Not the men of Edom only, but all the enemies of Jacob,
heathen as well as believing, shall be subject to the cruel
scourge that is to come. Sion shall witness their judgement,
and from Sion shall come the lasting peace. But Edom, chosen
though it had been, was doomed to dispossession.

Abdias has proved himself worthy of his place among the
prophets: the Edomites *were* dislodged from their lofty Petra,
and another nation, the Nabateans, occupied the moun-
tainous country they had left. Nobody seems to know when
this took place, but it is clear that in the time of Our Lord
when Herod was putting up defences around the stronghold
of Machaerus, the Nabateans, against whom he was arming
himself, had already been in possession of Petra. According
to the prophecy of Jeremias it would be the lot of Nabuchodonosor, the Chaldean king, to lead away Edom captive, and
assuming that this fell out as the prophet said it would, the
proud sons of Esau were not given long to digest Abdias'
warnings. It looks as if they suffered almost at once.

Where Edom fled to from Petra is again uncertain, but
Abdias was right when he said that the eagle would suffer
first at heathen hands and then be devoured as flaming stubble by her own flesh; Judas Machabeus, as it happened, was
the one to verify this latter forecast: he 'fought against the
children of Esau in Idumaea, and them that were in Acraba-
thane, because they beset the Israelites round about, and
he made a great slaughter of them.'[1]

Thus was the 'eagle that had set her nest among the stars'
brought low. From the sinister-looking crags in which she

[1] 1 Machab, v. 3.

dwelt, Edom had sneered down upon humanity too long. Year
after year she had watched the endless files of merchants and
pilgrims crawling along the gorge, and year after year she
had felt safer. Edom despised her fellow man. With the
broken country falling away from Petra for miles and miles
into the hot distance of piled-up purple hills, the sense of
right proportion might well endure decay. Where big things
appear small it is frequently the case that small things, mean
things, assume a bigness that is not theirs by right, and here
on this puckered tablecloth of pale brown, with man—the
greatest visible work of God—appearing as an ant, Edom's
perspectives went to bits. Edom was all that mattered. The
eagle Edom sat upon that landscape as if she had hatched it.
I think it is Chesterton who says somewhere that heights were
designed by God to be looked at, and not to be looked from;
and that the religion of the Scot was clearly invented by men
who dwelt on peaks. This is perhaps a little sweeping, but
certainly in the case of Edom, whether the geographical
setting affected it or not, a certain hardness of heart, a longing to revenge an ancient wrong, a jealousy that was altogether cruel, were the only results of the long estrangement
from the more sociable brother Jacob.

'Thou shalt not rejoice over the children of Juda in the
day of their destruction.' The eagle was losing its majesty in
its fierceness. Edom, hovering over that parched country, was
hovering now not so much as an eagle—which she would
have liked—but as a cuckoo . . . which was faintly ridiculous.
Having hatched in the nests of others, she could no longer
defend her own. Let her learn wisdom from the Book of the
Psalms: 'To *thee* have I lifted up my eyes, who dwellest in
the heavens.'[2]

[2] Ps. cxxii, 1.

V. Jonas: The Querulous

i

MANY other titles besides that of the 'querulous' might fittingly be applied to the extraordinary prophet before us. He could as well be thought of as 'the rebellious,' 'the faint-hearted,' the 'character' and even—dare we say it?—the 'comic.' This quicksilvery individual is a man of parts.

Though the Prophecy of Jonas is written in the third person, it is felt in the reading of it that the book is autobiographical; there are passages so revealing (the part that gives us God's dealings with the prophet as he sits under the withering ivy, for instance) that it is hard to believe that the work is not from the pen of the central figure. Assuming, then, that Jonas wrote the prophecy, it is only a pity that he did not tell us something more; he ends as abruptly as he begins, and all we know about him is what he did on his Ninive mission. This, the Ninive adventure, was evidently the one big happening of his life, but his was such a life that recordable incidents can hardly have been wanting— before as well as after the Ninive episode. That an Osee or an Amos should slip out of the pages of Holy Scripture the moment their message is delivered is not resented; we look upon them as being so close-knit in character with the word of God that as soon as the 'voice' is silent it is idle to pry further. With Jonas, however, the case is not the same; his is a career which we should like to follow to the death-bed —not because he is a hero (the others are far more heroic), but because he is such a complete identity as a man, apart altogether from what he is as a man of God.

Thus in some ways Jonas is seen to be the most tantalising of the Minor Prophets, rather because there is so much to go upon than because there is so little . . . much and then nothing. Even the penitent Ninive is left somewhat in mid-air. We have no further hint as to how far this quite appalling city went in its conversion, or as to how long the reform lasted; it was sorry and it was spared, and that is all we know.

As might be expected, legend is thick about the name of Jonas, as it is about the name of any startling personality. He is the son, we are told, of the widow of Sareptha (of Elias fame); he is the messenger of Elias; he is the anonymous prophet 'coming to the king of Israel [Achab]'; he is a number of unlikely and unnamed people, all of whom appear to make their claim at much the same period of history—around the time of Elias. This, incidentally, is quite consonant with the only mention of Jonas in the Old Testament apart from the prophecy which bears his name. In 4 Kings, chapter xiv, the 25th verse tells us that 'Jonas the son of Amathi' had been prophesying to good effect in the reign of Jeroboam the Second, son of Joas. Indeed there is something peculiarly happy in being able to link up the name of Jonas with that of Elias; they are quite definitely of one piece: obstinate, fugitive, perhaps a shade liverish—yet wildly attractive withal —brave as lions when once they have brought themselves to the point, and—in a gruff sort of way and on occasions— entirely self-sacrificing. It is from the older prophet, doubt-less, that Jonas gets his habit of praying for death when things go wrong. But we are anticipating.

If Jonas was of Geth Opher, as the author of 4 Kings says

he was, then Jonas belonged to the tribe of Zabulon and was a Galilean. Having foretold to Jeroboam his good fortune, without however stressing the ephemeral nature of it, 'the word of the Lord' came to him 'saying: Arise and go into Ninive the great city and preach in it; for the wickedness thereof is come before me.' But Jonas (and in the Galilean there is often that curious mixture of almost yokel simplicity—yielding to graciousness, blended with a sullen obstinacy—yielding to nothing at all) . . . but Jonas thought otherwise. Until it comes to saving life, Jonas, as we shall see, has none of the self-forgetting virtues. He could not forget himself, so he did his best to forget his prophetical vocation. 'And Jonas rose up to flee into Tharsis from the face of the Lord, and he went down to Joppe and found a ship going to Tharsis; and he paid the fare thereof and went down into it, to go with them to Tharsis from the face of the Lord.' We can feel for him; the prospect would have urged many a man to do the same. Up to now, Jonas had gone about his professional duties conscientiously enough, delivering soft messages in the silken ears of kings. This present duty was to be of quite a different order. A departure, so it seemed to Jonas, from what he felt to be his bent, and not at all a departure that he cared about. True, it was the signified will of God and there was no denying that, only it was not one of those acts of the Divine Will that Jonas was prepared to face. In that case he had better run away from it while the running was good. And the running *was* good as it happened: 'and he found a ship going to Tharsis . . .' No, Jonas at this point was certainly not a self-forgetting saint. Nor could he forget the rumours he had heard about Ninive. The evil fame of Assyria's capital, that city of fabulous riches and barbarous revelries, had spread even as far west as Samaria, and the thought of preaching penance in its midst was enough to strike the hottest gospeller with fear. Ninive, where they spoke a different language! Ninive, where the inhabitants were heathen—and what heathen! And he, Jonas, no hot-gospeller at best, to be Ninive's father-confessor! He, the sensitive Jonas, to be its blood-and-thunderer. It was unthinkable, he must look up routes elsewhere.

What of Tharsis?

Rumour had reached him of Tharsis also, telling him that this was a city more after his own heart: the people kindly, the climate mild . . . he would see if he could not visit Tharsis.

There are apparently three possible Tharsises to which Jonas may have purposed to sail: S. Paul's Tharsis in Cilicia; a Tharsis in Spain; and 'Tharsis' standing for 'Carthage'— Tunis of to-day. In the case of each, be it noted, the journey from Palestine would mean setting out in a westerly direction . . . and the Lord had bidden Jonas go east. If the prophet's mind was contrary, it might as well be clean contrary. He would go first of all to Joppe and see what could be done. Before we take our stock of the prophet on the landing-stage at Joppe we can remind ourselves that this is not the first time that a prophet of the Lord has differed from his God, though it is by far the most glaring instance of it.[1] Even the patriarch Moses begged to be excused, so far did he differ from the will of God. Any prophet, any leader, any reformer, has got to leap. That he will shrink from the work is inevitable and possibly even necessary to the work he is to do

[1] The name of Balaam suggests itself; admittedly the disobedience of this prophet is even more flagrant (and in his case also the Lord saw to it that His work was done eventually) , but one hardly feels that he deserves to be placed on quite the same footing as those of whom mention will be made and who were, in spite of hesitations, definitely on the side of the angels from the beginning.

(the Lord would scarcely choose the man who volunteered);
more, it is the price—the part of it at all events that seems to
cost the most—of success. What he has got to guard against
is running too far back to take his jump . . . and running
right away. Not only Moses, not only Elias, not only Jonas,
but all that have stood and shouted down the spirit of the age
in which they lived, have felt the soft, sensible, humility-
suggesting urge to give it up. Jonas fled from the voice of
God; Elias fled from the voice of God; Moses very nearly fled
from the voice of God. But because the Lord trusted His
servants more than they trusted themselves (and more than
they trusted Him), *and* because there was a certain work He
wanted done, excuses were not listened to, rebellious wills
were overridden, sloppy and even selfish decisions were re-
versed and a whole course of action was insisted on by God,
screwed down and sealed, so that the ghastly tragedy of a
spoiled saint or spoiled design in fact should not eventuate.
The prophets who vacillated and still were treated so were
fortunate; not all are free to play with grace; those who do
are made to pay, even though they yield completely in the
end: Moses . . . Elias . . . Jonas.

We, to whom the call is seldom to such heights of heroism
or depths of abnegation, have similar excuses up our sleeves,
based for the most part on profound 'unworthiness.' Unequal,
we say, to the leader's rôle; unsuited for so spiritual a work;
opposition, at this particular moment, and with people thinking as they do, would indicate that God wills otherwise . . .
and the rest. How often have we not heard, and said, this
kind of thing? Heavens above, it is the work of GOD. Is His
arm shortened because mine is weak? Would anything ever
have been done for God if men had gauged their God-sent
projects by their human powers? If there is one principle

more than another that finds a backing in Old Testament as
well as New, in the history of the Church as well as in the
history of each religious order or even saint, it is the principle
that opposition—whether from within or from without—is
not of itself a call to yield the day. But rather the reverse.
The more overwhelming the difficulties, very often, the more
certain it is, that the work is the work of God. The race to
God is an obstacle race . . . obstacle *and* race. It is hard
enough to get started, but once started, we run. To the objection that the best pace is the steadiest pace I answer that a
better pace still is a fast one. If the saints had listened to the
voice that urged a greater caution, a more discreet approach,
a less merciless treatment of self, they would, quite simply,
not have been saints. The same assertion that 'the truest fire
is the fire that lasts' did not, we may be sure. escape the ears
of the saints; nor were they never tempted to think the same
themselves. The principle, however, on which they acted
seems to have been that the truest fire was the fire that burned.
The love of God, like God Himself, is a 'consuming fire.'

Few indeed are found worthy to inherit the blessing reserved for those who 'suffer reproach for the name of Christ,'
but even if straightforward persecution is absent from the
lives of those who in a humbler way attempt the works of
God, opposition—cold, damp, smothering, devitalizing opposition—will have to be faced. Opposition which is all the more
deadening because of the quarter from which it comes, the
reputable quarter; and all the more unnerving because of the
weapons employed, the weapons of peace. So well attested are
the arguments, so thick with texts the silky persuasions, that
nothing but the sheer grace of God can hold the ground. 'Cast
all your care on Him,' says S. Peter (who, with the experience
behind him of having attempted to walk on the water and of

having succeeded in supporting the Church, is qualified to speak about trust), 'cast all your care on Him, for He hath care of you.'

Read the First Book of Esdras, chapters iii to vi, and speculate with trembling what would have happened if Zorobabel had burked the issue. If Zorobabel had melted before the blaze of malice or the glare of sickening publicity, would God have forced him to it? Would the Lord have taken him by the scruff of the neck, as we shall see Him doing with Jonas in a minute, and forced his face among the weeds and heaped-up stones that was the ruins of Jerusalem and told him 'Build'? He might have done, we do not know; at all events we cannot count on being treated so ourselves. God gives us a work to do; it meets with opposition, it starts, and meets with setback; it goes on . . . and fails. A pity we ever started? No! We have given ourselves for the work of God; we meet the opposition; we meet the setbacks; we meet the failure . . . and not till then, not till it has been proved that failure was what God wanted all along, do we retire. And why? Because then, and then only, have we won. We have handed back finished what He wanted us to do. The fact that it was not finished in our way but in His will not disqualify the work. We have been 'users' only . . . used *to use* His tools . . . and what is there to complain of in that? With the broken tools in our hands we come to render account . . . here they are, back again where they belong . . . they have been selfishly used perhaps, mistakenly used, clumsily used, but anyway *used,* and if the net result is failure, well and good.

No need to go so far away as Esdras. If Zorobabel's flaming courage fails to stir, we have only to look among the saints. Zorobabel restored a ruined city, others have restored a ruined Rule. (The reforming saints certainly, but the founders them-

selves of religious orders were many of them Zorobabels.)
But be the man founder, reformer, prophet, or chosen instrument of God, it is opposition even more than physical suffering that will wear him thin. The secret of S. John of the
Cross, S. Bruno, S. Ignatius, S. John of God and the rest was
not that they believed that it was high time something were
done, or that *they* were capable of doing it, but rather that
whatever God wanted done, *He* was capable of bringing
about—even out of material such as they. And that that being
so, nothing, absolutely nothing, could be suffered to interfere.
God's countermand alone had power to stay their hands. How
else can we account for the adamantine obstinacy of the saints
in getting what they wanted for their Rules? For them the
problem resolved itself into the practical question as to what
God wanted of them next, and then the duty was to persevere.
Perseverance, like other 'crowning virtues,' is only measurable
by going on—going on persevering. And if nothing is to show
for all the toil, the effort will bear fruit for someone else.
Time, to those whose hope is real, can be lost sight of altogether, insured as it is by fidelity to the 'now.'

'And therefore *we* also, having so great a cloud of witnesses
over our head,'[2] ought not to be puzzled or saddened when a
frozen wall of resistance comes between our groping hands
and God. We are in the tradition. He to whom we first
stretched out with our prayers of self-dedication can do away
in the twinkling of an eye with human limitations, 'impossible' circumstances and 'reasonable' hostility. The weak
things of this world are always God's choice wherever there
is to be a confounding of the strong; the branch, if it is to bear
fruit, must be purged; the seed, if it grow, must die.

Who would have thought that Margaret Mary from her

[2] Heb. xii, 1.

convent, and Colombière from his court, could between them
have moved the world? Or that Lourdes could have risen
triumphant from the assertions, however dogged, of a four-
teen-year-old peasant, Bernadette? And it must always be so
in a Body which has risen from a Tomb. We have not heard
the last, I hope, of Charles de Foucauld and of what he did
for God; a prophet whose dreams were still-born, a founder
who founded nothing, a reformer who reformed himself, a
failure . . . as far as he could see.

Ah yes, it is easy enough now for us to know the truth that
is contained in failure—we who have the Crucifix before
our eyes; glad can we be 'to suffer something for the name of
Jesus'; we have 'the mind of Christ' and need not dread a
failure in His cause. But not so they.

ii

'And he went down to Joppe and found a ship.' Arrived
at the water's edge he was able to roam the expanse of blue
with a meditative eye. He had probably never seen the sea
before, and now the sight and sound and smell of it were
additional spurs to the pace he was setting himself. This at
last was adventure. If Jonas had cared to look into his interior, as the handbooks of the spiritual life would have
urged him to do at this momentous juncture, he would have
found much to cause him acute misgiving; but Jonas was in
holiday mood, and nothing on earth just then would have
induced him to interrupt his pacing of the quay for the
searching exercise of a particular *examen*. Jonas was—if one
may use the expression—'quit of all that.' He had discarded
his prophetical garment of skin and hair (the official uniform,
as it were, of the man of God); his beard had been trimmed
at one of the little booths that supplied the needs of mer-

chants newly come to port; he had fed generously at one of
the many waterside *khans*—the kind of not very respectable
tavern that is more than adequately represented in the har-
bours of every age and nation—and was feeling equal, though
not perhaps eager, to the task of shaking for ever the dust of
Palestine from off his feet.

'He found a ship going to Tharsis . . . paid the fare thereof
and went down into it.' We can picture the whilom man of
God, moving from group to group and from boat to boat,
listening with an unpractised ear to the loose talk and unfamiliar accent of these sea-faring roughs, scum, for the most
part, from all over the Mediterranean world. He must pick
up many hints if he is to keep secret the calling he has followed hitherto. There is no great risk that he will be recognized so far from home, but better choose a heathen crew
while he is about it. There is not much difficulty in that! So
with a show of boldness and a confidence overdone, Jonas,
his leather money-belt safely hidden in the folds of his flow-
ing *talith*, makes towards a craft that more than any other
flaunts the emblems of the gods. Even if, as the text seems to
suggest, his first and second enquiry failed to obtain for Jonas
what he wanted, he found in the end a vessel whose shipping
could, for a consideration, include the town he sought. An
expectant one-time prophet boards the little schooner in the
late afternoon; a bundle of newly-acquired clothing is under
his arm and a crate of provisions—he has made a point of
selecting 'unclean' foods—is carried in his train. There is a
light breeze, and the sound of tiny waves lapping the sides
of the ship is as soothing music to the fugitive. He hears with
equal pleasure the jingling of brasses as the twitching and
flapping of sails disturb the hundred little pagan gods.

It is indeed delightful to be setting out thus on a voyage

of chance (though he little knows what chances the Lord will employ) after the dull dusty round of the somewhat provincial life in Israel. There is a lot to be said for independence. The merchant on a holiday, thinks Jonas, is a vastly more satisfactory being than the prophet on a mission, and as the shore recedes and the boat makes away into the crimson of the setting sun, Jonas congratulates himself on his decision. They pass the smaller fishing-boats, gay with bunches of flowers at the bows, bobbing up and down on the sparkling water; they can hear the creak of rowing and the splash of oars. Jonas is conscious that the evening air is sending ripples along his silken shoulders; that the voices of men singing over their nets on the shore are getting fainter; that the sun behind him has dipped into the sea, sweeping up with it the light from the opposite hills . . . and that the last threads that bind him to the land are wearing thin. Jonas makes a move to go below, and in the regal hush of dusk a star comes out to gleam above the prophet's head.

iii

How long they had been afloat before the next incident, the storm, took place we do not know. It looks as though the sailors had had time to form a rough estimate of their singular companion, but that they were puzzled as to what his business was and where he came from. That Jonas had managed to cover up his profession is hardly a surprise to us, but that his nationality remained a secret is astonishing, seeing the man was a Jew and must have looked it.

One wonders how long, in a changeable moody person like Jonas, the feeling of having successfully resisted Providence would have lasted. With the hours of leisure hanging on his hands, Jonas would have been hard put to it to exclude the thought of God. That he managed to do so is never even hinted at in the text. What with the sea to act as the mirror of God's majesty and the sky to mantle the grandest of His works, Jonas, sitting in the bows and trying to think of Tharsis, must have suffered uncomfortable distractions. The words he had so often recited from the Psalms would have occurred to his mind: 'they that go down to the sea in ships, doing business in the great waters, these have seen the works of the Lord, and his wonders in the deep.'[3] If the prophet was at all like the rest of us, the early bravado which his defiance had lent him would have gradually ebbed away, and we can think of Jonas—on about his third day on the water— as the victim of his temperament: he feels that he is being looked at with sullen suspicion by the men; he hates to catch himself mechanically breathing prayers; he finds that the diet disagrees with him, and that there has been wisdom behind the Hebrew ban on certain foods; he can no longer derive the smallest entertainment from listening to the sailors' conversation: endless and mendacious accounts of amorous escapades ashore. Taken all in all he will be glad when these great blue foam-streaked waves will wash him up on the Tharsis shore. Tharsis will give him music, lights, fires and sticky sweets to take his mind from the disquieting thought of God.

The mariners, had they looked up from their tightening of ropes against the coming storm, would have noticed that the step of the foreign gentleman, as he made his way below, had lost its spring.

The livestock were made fast—trussed up like bunches of

[3] Ps. cvi, 23, 24. (It is thought that this psalm was composed during the Captivity—so Neale and Littledale—in which case Jonas would *not* have been reminded of it, but since the dates of most of the later psalms are disputed, it can reasonably be quoted here.)

celery—and bellowing as though they knew what was in store; the hurricane sheets were dragged out; the gods were invoked . . . a soft breeze blew up suddenly across the waste and after a few preliminary jerkings and flappings filled each sail as a skin is filled with wine. And Jonas, he who had stepped so debonair upon the Joppe shore, flung himself heavily upon his bunk and wished for death.

iv

'But the Lord sent a great wind into the sea, and a great tempest was raised in the sea and the ship was in danger to be broken. And the mariners were afraid, and the men cried to their god; and they cast forth the wares that were in the ship into the sea to lighten it of them; and Jonas went down into the inner part of the ship and fell into a deep sleep.' The passage puts us at once into just that attitude of expectancy that only a really gifted writer can achieve in a few words. The storm, it makes a point of telling us, is no ordinary gale: it was raised for a purpose. Even the sailors, hard-bitten, salt-crusted men that they were, saw this and were afraid. We can see the bales of cloth, the crates of fruit, ship's furniture and private belongings, junk of every sort . . . everything tumbled overboard in the confusion of fear. And Jonas went to bed and slept!

'And the ship-master came to him and said to him: Why art thou fast asleep? Rise up, call upon thy God, if so be that God will think of us that we may not perish.' It is here that stern theologians and solemn divines pause in their sifting of the text to tell us how atrophying to the conscience is the state of sin. Danger, they advance, threatening on every side, and the soul, insensible, is at rest within. That is so, and it is one of the tragedies that a priest is constantly called upon to

witness: how satisfied some people can be who have the least
reason to feel secure. But may we not take it here that the
slumber of Jonas was profound, not because he had an easy
mind (we have cast doubt upon that above), but because he
had an empty stomach? We learn from the text that the
prophet 'went down' after the storm had got well under
way, and *not* that he was asleep when it began. Is it so surprising that Jonas slept when the gale was at its height? There is
nothing so exhausting as seasickness, and the prophet, at sea
for the first time, had in all probability been horribly ill. It
is more than likely that his conscience *was* inoperative at the
time, but experience seems to show that the condition induced by a rough passage is of itself inclined to banish the
thought of God, and of sin, and of everything else . . .
whether the voyager is fleeing from the face of the Lord or
doing his best to remain in His presence. In any case Jonas
slept.

While the captain was below, trying by turns to coax and
bully a reluctant prophet into an attitude of prayer, the
sailors on deck were busy in consultation as to why the gods
had thus afflicted them. 'And they said every one to his fellow:
Come and let us cast lots that we may know why this evil is
upon us. And they cast lots, and the lot fell upon Jonas.' As
so often happens on board ship the meeting decided upon a
lottery. Jonas was revealed as being the cause of all the
trouble. He was sent for. We can see the poor pale prophet
as his head and shoulders rise above the opening of the hatch,
his lovely clothes flung on anyhow, his beard and hair disturbed. He looks wretched. He had thought that by hiding
himself downstairs he could rid himself of the staring crew;
he had thought that by pretending to pray he could rid himself of this exasperating captain; he had thought that by going

to sleep again he could rid himself of God. And here he was, climbing on deck in his bare feet, summoned as if to a jury, and having to face crew, captain, and in all probability God as well. It was a little hard . . . and he who had been so ill below.

'And they said to him: Tell us for what cause this evil is upon us; what is thy business? of what country art thou? and whither goest thou? and of what people art thou? We can hear the questions being shot at the man from different mouths as the prophet is flung, partly by the motion of the waves and partly by the roughness of the men, from one to another of the group. The ropes creak, the water eddies round his ankles, great gusts of wind threaten to lift him bodily into the sea by his billowing silks. He clings to whatever his hand can hold; everything is wet. In his ears there is the confused roar of breaking wave, of moaning cattle, of tearing gale, and of questioning sailor. Jonas wishes he had never resisted the voice of God. Jonas wishes for Tharsis . . . for Joppe . . . for Ninive even . . . for *death* . . . for anything, in fact, but this.

'And he said to them: I am a Hebrew and I fear the Lord the God of heaven, who made both the sea and the dry land' —and how lovingly must not Jonas have lingered over the last two words—'and the men were greatly afraid and they said to him: Why hast thou done this? . . . What shall we do to thee that the sea may be calm to us? for the sea flowed and swelled.' It is here that I must admit defeat: for myself I cannot decide whether it was that Jonas rose to the occasion in this moment of crisis (as the commentators without exception seem to have decided that he did) or whether a loophole presented itself as a final means of escape. Did he want to save the others or did he hope to drown himself? In any case he was in a position where he could afford to be reckless, and

he was. 'And he said to them'—with a last desperate flourish
we may be sure—'Take me up and cast me into the sea, and
the sea shall be calm to you; for I know that for my sake this
great tempest is upon you.' Even if Jonas had hoped to be
saved by the Lord, even if—as is far more likely—he hoped
to die and be saved *from* the Lord, the offer was a magnificent
one. And the magnificence impressed the crew. One feels that
if they had been French or Italian the sailors, frightened
though they were, would have tossed their caps in the air and
cheered. 'And the men rowed hard to return to the land but
they were not able'; 'dug the sea' is the Revised Version's
happier wording. The sailors were determined to avoid, if it
were humanly possible to do so, the expedient suggested by
the prophet's generosity. Jonas has arrived. Jonas has succeeded thus far, his prestige is re-established; the swaggering
stranger of the Joppe pier has proved himself after all; an
indifferent sailor he may be, but his heroism is unquestioned.
And there he is in his bright colours striking attitudes on the
deck (with difficulty enough, seeing he would have had to
hold on to this and that to keep his balance), a brave figure
and a picturesque, though a little the worse for his recent ills.

A point to notice[4] is how well the unbelieving sailor be-
haves throughout the whole story. There is the shipmaster
with his injunctions to pray; there are the men with their
supernatural view of the storm and their horror that it
should be traceable to a Hebrew; the ship's company as a
whole with its unwillingness to throw the culprit overboard;
and finally the united prayer, not to their gods, but to the
Lord. 'And they cried to the Lord and said: We beseech thee,
O Lord, let us not perish for this man's life, and lay not upon

[4] For this and for the whale portion of the story, see Farrar (op. cit., pp.
238, 239) who is unexpectedly to the point, both in his opinions and in the
authorities he cites.

us innocent blood, for thou, O Lord, hast done as it pleased thee.'

There was nothing for it, the sinful Hebrew must suffer for his sin; it was the will of the Hebrew God, and it would certainly, if the prophet had heard the voice aright, save the rest. They would pray therefore for all concerned, and commit the sinner to the deep. Sadly, gently, fondly, Jonas is bidden farewell and led to the vessel's side, 'and they cast him into the sea, and the sea ceased from raging.' And before the writer goes on to tell of the prophet's fate, he gives the news that all on board 'sacrificed victims to the Lord' and 'made vows.' So whatever else the attempted escape effected, there was one good thing to show for Jonas' having taken ship and fled.

v

'Now the Lord prepared a very great fish to swallow up Jonas, and Jonas was in the belly of the fish three days and three nights.' This verse has given rise to more derision than almost any other verse in Sacred Scripture. Once granted that miracles *do* take place, there seems not the smallest grounds for denying this one. If God can exist in a tabernacle (and purity in a slum) then man can exist in a whale. Left to myself I should probably have given to man a less noble beast and to God a more worthy shrine; as it is, I would merely pause before going on with the story to observe that Our Lord alluded to the whale incident on two separate occasions, and in neither case did He so much as hint that He was referring to an allegory.[5]

[5] Fr. Pope draws attention to the fact that 'there are no whales in the Mediterranean where Jonas met his fate; hence it is always well to speak of Jonas' host as a "big fish."' Op. cit., p. 378.

'And Jonas prayed to the Lord his God out of the belly of the fish.' The short second chapter is the prayer he prayed. It is a good prayer, full of an exquisite thanksgiving, in which he says—and one would not have guessed the fact from the previous chapter—that 'when my soul was in distress within me I remembered the Lord.' He tells of the hope that no amount of waves can quench or fishes swallow up; his life will, he knows, be 'brought up from corruption, O Lord my God . . . and I shall see thy holy temple yet again. . . .' Considering where he was situated at the time, this was no mean act of faith. 'But I with the voice of praise,' he continues, 'will sacrifice to thee; I will pay whatsoever I have vowed, for my salvation to the Lord.' And as soon as the Lord has heard *that,* He 'spoke to the fish'—delightful picture— 'and it vomited out Jonas upon the dry land.' Wonderful indeed it is that Our Lord should choose so designedly playful a passage in Holy Scripture, playful if not very nearly *funny,* to exemplify one of His most solemn utterances. To the crew, the swallowing up of Jonas could hardly have been more final. Christ's Resurrection was to follow upon an ending that was every bit as hopeless. Thus the sailors in the Prophecy returning to their posts, the Apostles in the Gospel hiding from the Jews, the little band of Christians saying their prayers in Diocletian's reign, the Fathers of the Society going on with their supper after the Brief of Suppression had been read at the Gesu[6] . . . they are all of a piece. 'Wherefore lift up the hands which hang down and the feeble knees . . . accounting that God is able to raise up even from the dead.'[7]

[6] 14 August, 1773.　　　　[7] Cf. Heb. xi, xii.

vi

There is nothing to tell us what land it was upon whose dry shores the prophet was washed. Once on his feet again, Jonas received the command of the Lord a second time, and this he obeyed like a lamb: 'And Jonas arose and went to Ninive according to the word of the Lord . . . and he cried and said: Yet forty days and Ninive shall be destroyed.' Notice that the prophecy is unconditional: there is no 'unless you shall do penance for your sins'; there is no invitation to dwell upon the thought of God—Jonas takes it for granted that Ninive knows nothing about Him. There is no hope held out whatever: forty days will see the end of Ninive and that is all there is about it.

From what we have already seen of Jonas we can make a fair guess that as he stood to preach in Ninive his thoughts were not unmixed with fear. No amount of repentant zeal could have blinded his eyes to the danger. If you want to know what the people of Ninive were like, turn over three pages of the Bible and the prophet Nahum will give you, in his second and third chapters, something on which to build a picture of their kind. Ninive was as cruel as it was lecherous, as godless as it was wealthy; no good could come of Ninive and Jonas expected none. The prophet resigned himself— with no great effort—to death, and was glad of the chance to be suffering it in the name of the Lord rather than under the matchboarding of a wrecked vessel. He told himself that he was the last person in the world for this kind of thing, but that no doubt he deserved it, and that in any case he would do his best.

And then to find that he was being listened to! And that

he was doing it uncommonly well. And that he was enjoying it.

Jonas is the complete fire-eating Amos of a decade later, with all the same enthusiasm and fewer words. The rabble, first of all, show signs of being moved, and then the fashionable quarter lends an ear. Jonas is much in demand, required to speak his single message in the halls of the great, and finally in the court itself. At last, when he has won the two extremes, the small shopkeeper comes running to his feet, and with him the struggling advocate, the humble schoolmaster and the itinerant scribe. And no mere flash-in-the-pan conversion either; Ninive goes about its reforms as it goes about its revels: it 'believed God,' it 'put on sackcloth from the greatest even to the least,' it 'proclaimed a fast.' Even the king himself was no exception, 'he rose up out of his throne, and cast away his robe from him, and was clothed with sackcloth and sat in ashes.' The people of Ninive had never heard of sackcloth as a material for clothing before; Jonas wore it, so would they. Jonas strewed ashes, they would sit in them. They looked to the prophet for everything, and Jonas, as always, rose to the occasion. It was a far cry from this to the swashbuckling Jonas of the Joppe quay; now he was the ascetic again, this man of many parts, preaching away in his shirt of penance, a staff in his hand and a girdle of leather about his waist.

We know what happened: man and beast were made to fast in the wild hope that 'God will turn and forgive, and will turn away from his fierce anger, and we shall not perish.' The hope was as wildly justified: 'God saw their works, that they were turned from their evil way, and God had mercy with regard to the evil that he said he would do to them, and he did it not.' Ninive had heard Jonas and God heard

Ninive. One wonders if the Ninives of to-day would ever obey a prophet's voice. Will they ever *hear* a prophet's voice? 'The harvest indeed is great but the labourers are few. Pray ye therefore the Lord of the harvest that he send forth labourers into the harvest.' Perhaps He has sent harvesters, sleeping harvesters, who have dreamed to the drone of the motor-reaper. The Lord of the harvest Himself tells us how His labourers are to work, 'carrying neither purse, nor scrip, nor shoes. . . .'[8] We talk much about the conversion of England, and we pray for it, too, please God, but only when we have learned to 'salute no man by the way'—least of all the rich man who keeps open house to the clergy but not to God —shall we be able to say with the seventy-two: 'Lord, the devils also are subject to us in thy name.' Prayer . . . poverty . . . fasting . . . thus, and thus only, shall the harvest be gathered.[9] And that is the tragedy of it. Perhaps He has sent us prophets, perhaps we ourselves have seen what prophets and kings of other times have desired to see and have not seen; perhaps we and our prophets have alike saluted the hospitable worldling once too often . . . and have feared to 'say to the sick in whatsoever city' we have entered that the 'Kingdom of God is come nigh to you'; perhaps we have indeed said: 'Peace to this house,' but added nothing about the price of it, '. . . Yea, peace to this house, prosperity and

8 Luke x, 2, 3, 4, 10, 11, 17.
9 'Frances of the Mother of God used to pray for the conversion of sinners, and especially for those in England. "The Lord told me," she relates, "that He was willing to give me three, and that it would not cost me my life, but that He wished me to wear a hair shirt for three days, and also to fast three days on bread and water. Some time later three English people came to make their abjuration in our Church. As soon as I entered the choir, Our Lord said to me: 'I am faithful to My promises, and you have not yet finished what I commanded you to do.' I had still one day's fast to make and I accomplished it that day." ' Saudreau. *Divine Communications*, Vol. II, p. 20.

plenty.' If we have, let us listen to what Jeremias has to say of our fathers who have done the same: 'From the least of them even to the greatest, all are given to covetousness; and from the prophet even to the priest, all are guilty of deceit . . . saying: Peace, peace, and there was no peace.'[10] Perhaps it can be said of our present-day prophets what Ezechiel says of Juda's: 'they have daubed them [the people of Jerusalem] without tempering the mortar.'[11]

Jonas, for all his faults, tempered not the mortar; nor did John the Baptist; nor did Our Lord and Saviour, Jesus Christ.[12]

vii

Jonas, with weeping Ninive at his feet and with no immediate prospects of a catastrophe, 'was exceedingly troubled and was angry; and he prayed to the Lord and said: I beseech thee, O Lord, is not this what I said when I was yet in my own country? Therefore I went before to flee into Tharsis, for I know that thou art a gracious and merciful God, patient and of much compassion, and easy to forgive evil. And now, O Lord, I beseech thee take my life from me, for it is better for me to die than to live.'

It should be refreshing, I suppose, to find how human the prophets are, but it should be equally humiliating to find how petty human nature can be. Jonas is frankly sorry that Ninive has been spared; he is not 'troubled' at having preached in vain—he knew that he had been a great success— he was 'troubled' at being *thought* to have preached in vain. The forty days were up, and Jonas was looking foolish.

When the prophet says in the above outbreak that he had

[10] Jer. vi, 14.   [11] Ezech. xxii, 28.
[12] Matt. iii, 2; iv, 7; Luke xiii, 3, 5.

suspected as much all along, he is certainly not giving the real reason for his attempted escape. As far as one can see it was fear of failure that had driven him to Joppe, not fear of success. 'Gracious and merciful . . . patient and of much compassion . . . and easy to forgive. . . .' Jonas had every reason to speak feelingly of these attributes of God, but they only irritated him now, now that they were being brought to bear upon his flock. 'Let me die,' goes on this petulant prophet in as many words, 'you are so ready to forgive that whatever I tell these Ninivites, you only play me false; it is no good my going on . . . much better let me die.' But even prophets must learn that death is one of those things that must be left to God. We may often have occasion to say that, all things considered, it were better for us to die, but the occasions only prove that the 'all things' have been 'considered' humanly. Explain to God and ask for light, but do not say that it is 'better' for you to die. For if it were, you would be dead. Let it be said for those who have a grudge against their lives that even the holiest have prayed to die—Tobias, Job, and (again) Elias in the Old Testament, and many a saint in the New—and for my part I have never managed to believe that their desire was *simply* to see the face of God; the Jonas, wearied of well-doing, saddened by sin, was surely lurking in the best of them.[13]

'And the Lord said: Dost thou think thou hast reason to be angry?' The Lord understands his peevish Jonas. There is no open rebuke such as we might expect from a God who can thunder from the mountain-top, no calling to order of a son, who after all has spoken very rudely; merely a gentle

[13] Strange that there are those who shrink from the bare thought of birth-control, yet who long for the conscience that admits of hastening death (their own). Death-control may well become the evil of a generation even more jaded than our own.

reminder of the justice or injustice of the thing, as between man and man, and that in the form of a question.

'Then Jonas went out of the city and sat towards the east side . . . and he made himself a booth there, and he sat under it in the shadow till he might see what should befall the city.' Without answering the Lord's question, and feeling he must somehow relieve the strain, Jonas goes for a short walk. It is evening (we know that from the verses that follow) and it is hot (or he would not have chosen the east side of the city—the sun was setting on the west). He finds a suitable place from which he can watch the city, and where if necessary he can sleep the night. But even in this weather the nights can be cold, so he makes a shelter. In getting together the sticks and bits of matting, rags and whatnot left beside the road, his mind is occupied, but when he sits down it is a piqued and jaundiced prophet that reviews his world. The last of his 'forty days' is closing in, and Jonas sits and waits 'that he might see what should befall the city.' There is just a chance, he tells himself, even now. How often in the last weeks has he not pictured to himself the fall of Ninive! He had wondered if it would come in the form of fire from heaven . . . an earthquake? . . . or a flood (he had hoped not, swirling waters brought back bitter memories) . . . would it be a plague? (he had pictured himself as the selfless untiring minister of a stricken people) . . . or was it to be merely an invasion? . . . and now it had all come to this . . . come to nothing. We can see the poor disgruntled man of God peering into the gloom as night closes in, and hating every separate light that stares at him from Ninive; he screws his weary lids in one last prayer, a prayer of fierce intensity and heat . . . perhaps the Lord at this eleventh hour will sweep away the city from his eyes.

Eventually Jonas slept. We can pass over the pain that his waking would have caused him; how the first sight that would meet his eyes would be the lovely city of Ninive, gleaming and solid under a shimmering veil of blue; how the distant buzz of early morning traffic would seem to challenge the spell his words had cast; how the glittering domes would mock him, flaunting their gold; how the stout buttressed wall proclaimed the city's permanence. As the prophet lay there in his booth, clenching and unclenching in his hands little wisps of yellow grass, a new life, the supernatural life, was being shaped by God in one of the wickedest cities in the world. But Jonas cared for none of it.

'And the Lord prepared an ivy, and it came up over the head of Jonas to be a shadow over his head and to cover him (for he was fatigued) and Jonas was exceeding glad of the ivy.' We come now to the last phase of the story. The Lord had more in mind than the calming down of a prophet who was being difficult. He was preparing an object-lesson for Jonas—much as He had prepared a series of little object-lessons on Mount Horeb for Jonas' master, Elias.[14] With a creeper rapidly spreading over his makeshift hut, the prophet had good reason to be glad; if spiritual consolations were wanting, at least there was here the balm afforded by the creature. Nature was giving him the green that soothed and the leaf that cast a shadow. 'But God prepared a worm when the morning arose on the following day, and it struck the ivy and it withered. And when the sun was risen, the Lord commanded a hot and burning wind; and the sun beat upon the head of Jonas and he broiled with the heat'— this is surely autobiographical, the writer is still on the verge of complaint when recording the events years later—'and he

[14] 3 Kings xix.

desired for his soul that he might die.' (Death is becoming an obsession; he will mention it again in a minute.)

We have seen that the ivy was not a delicate attention, we shall see now that it was not a practical joke.

'And the Lord said to Jonas: Dost thou think thou hast reason to be angry for the ivy? and he said: *I am angry with reason even unto death.* And the Lord said: Thou art grieved for the ivy for which thou hast not laboured nor made to grow, which in one night came up and in one night perished. And shall not I spare Ninive, that great city in which there are more than a hundred and twenty thousand persons that know not how to distinguish between their right hand and their left, and many beasts.'

The Lord, infinitely 'gracious'—to use the prophet's word —infinitely 'easy to forgive,' repeats the question He has asked before and this time Jonas answers it: 'I am angry with reason even unto death.' It is characteristic, but at least it is frank. 'I am not angry about the ivy particularly; I am not angry about Ninive any more; I am just angry.' One loves Jonas for this confession. How often have we not felt that life was responsible for anger, not this or that, but sheer disappointment-bringing, colour-lacking, reason-ridden, *life* ... and that obviously death was the only thing worth sighing for. In Jonas' admission there is the hint of regret; he seems to see that the service of God requires a gallantry to which he cannot rise; he feels that he will never learn what lies behind the acts of God; he admits that storms, penitent cities, withered ivies, broiling heats, are all part and parcel of a system he does not understand. Give him death and he will cause no more trouble.

In justice to Jonas let us remind ourselves that the man was worn out. He had preached a forty days' mission, giving out nervous energy and receiving unlooked-for applause. All this had suddenly ceased and there was a purely physical reaction. Add to that his tendency to live in the extremes of either elation or depression, together with the disappointments of the last twenty-four hours, and you have a very exhausted Jonas. Even if we give him a period of rest between the storm at sea and the missionary enterprise, we have to allow for the effects of the long journey east, travelling uncomfortably and as a foreigner. Jonas had had a tiring year and many a more generous man would have surely felt as sour.

Very often it is when body and soul are weary—apathetic almost—that God chooses to send His brightest lights. Perhaps it is because then there is nothing else in the mind to offer resistance or counter-attraction; the whole organism is spent, and so, in a sense, receptive. It cuts both ways because temptation as well as grace is listened to. When in some such condition, then, Jonas received the lesson of a lifetime, a lesson he had not fully learned from the more forcible lesson of the 'big fish.' The withered ivy and the rescued city: the prestige of a man and the salvation of thousands! Our Lord's words to the 'son of thunder' might well have been said to Jonas: 'you know not of what spirit you are.' It was not enough that the Power of God should be preached by His apostles, His Toleration must be given equal place. Jonas was shown a view of Ninive he had not seen before, he saw it supported by the hand that had created its inhabitants, the hand that had raised its walls to shelter them, the same hand that had caused to grow, and then to fade, the plant whose shrivelled leaves were being blown about his feet . . . (by that same 'hot wind' that the Lord had sent). 'Is thy eye evil because I am good?' Jonas was invited to rise above himself and see things as they really were—set one beside the other in the sight of God.

Of Jonas, alas, we know no more. We hope that he rose up from where he was sitting, that he shook the dust from the folds of his tunic, that he covered his tanned and 'broiling' scalp, and that he wandered off in the direction of the city with a new wisdom in his heart and words of congratulation on his lips. We are familiar by now with the *mals du pays,* and may be sure that they were not lacking here: the cracked earth that seemed to strike at the soles of the prophet's feet, the grasshoppers that flicked in the silence, the hot air that seemed to weigh on his chest like a poultice . . . all these incidental rubs the prophet had to put up with, but if Jonas had learned what the Lord had been at such pains to explain, the prophet's soul was a-song as he faced the midday heats. Flight? . . . dear Lord, no! . . . Death? . . . dear Lord, no! . . . a purified Ninive? . . . dear Lord, why not? 'Non moriar sed vivam, et narrabo opera Domini.'[15]

[15] Ps. cxvii, 17.

VI. Micheas: The Morasthite

I HAVE no great contribution to make towards the literature of Micheas. Let us face the seven chapters bravely and confess that his is not the prophecy that grips us most.

Though of all the Minor Prophets the least individual, Micheas is yet the most representative. Even Joel, in spite of what we have called his 'cosmic' qualities and the many likenesses he bears to other prophets, is not such a typical seer as is this present. Micheas, though we know very little about the man, exactly embodies for us the idea 'prophet'; he foretells—with both foreboding and forepromise; he resembles the arch-prophet Isaias so nearly as to make quotation from memory inadvisable, and his Messianic emphasis is such that the prophecy is both tempered with gentleness and raised in dignity to rank with the most important. He is the perfect model of what a prophet ought to be.

Micheas prophesied under Joatham, Achaz, and Ezechias (roughly therefore between 750 and 700 B.C.) and was the only one of the group we are dealing with who can be shown to have worked in Juda as well as Israel. In this respect he is the Maurice Baring of the Minor Prophets, glad to be the product of rival kingdoms. But in this respect only, since Micheas, like Amos, is a herdsman, a humble son of the low-lying flats of Philistia. Himself a Morasthite, he 'saw the word concerning Samaria and Jerusalem' and having told us that, he gives us nothing more. For further details of Micheas' life we have to look elsewhere, and then we can trace only a single incident connected with his name. It is Jeremias who provides us with the information when he relates how, by his ability to quote precedent in the shape of Micheas's immunity, he escaped death under similar circumstances. 'Micheas of Morasthi,' says Jeremias, 'was a prophet in the days of Ezechias king of Juda, and he spoke to all the people of Juda saying: Thus saith the Lord of hosts: Sion shall be ploughed as a field and Jerusalem shall be a heap of stones . . .' which was no less after all than what he, Jeremias, had said . . . and 'did Ezechias and all Juda,' he asks, 'condemn him to death? Did they not fear the Lord?'[1] So Jeremias was spared, and it says something for the right-mindedness of his captors that he was. We can hardly see Amasias going back on his sentence had Amos remembered a text or two from Isaias. Before leaving the incident, Jeremias adds that his forerunner's preaching had been eminently successful.

It has been hinted above that Micheas and Isaias have many points in common, and this is especially the case towards the close of the Major Prophet's book; the critics seem to make Isaias the earlier of the two, but the change in Isaias' style and language to meet the Messianic theme is sufficiently marked to warrant the tentative suggestion that, though senior in years and longer—if one may say it with respect—'on the bookstalls,' he may have borrowed from the lesser luminary, Micheas. Whether they received inspiration from one another or not, and if so whether Isaias from Micheas or Micheas from Isaias, are questions for the experts to decide. One thing is tolerably certain and that is that Isaias and Micheas were more or less contemporaries. That the major and the minor prophet knew each other personally is not

[1] Jer. xxxvi, 18.

likely: Isaias was of the blood royal, Micheas was the least of men. If the former started life in his grandfather's court (as a fairly reliable tradition says he did), very different was the upbringing of the latter. Micheas does not give his father's name, and this omission is taken as evidence of the prophet's humble lineage, but even if we had nothing else to guide us, the whole tenor of the prophecy is such that the author's interests are seen to be of the people as much as his sympathies are with them.

We are not surprised, then, to find that it is the misuse of wealth and the worldliness of the priests that are the first objects of the prophet's onslaught; throughout the whole work indeed, Micheas is seen to feel deepest where oppression of the poor calls for censure. Thus we see in this prophet very much that we have seen in Amos, only the manner of expression is not the same; both refer the bad state of the two nations to the worship of false gods (but do not make idolatry their central theme), both reproach their public with ingratitude, and both expose the evils of sensuality. But where Amos and Micheas are most agreed is in their outspoken— though differently spoken—hatred of despotism. Which makes it all the more extraordinary that Micheas was not killed. Perhaps as a prophet he was too closely identified with Isaias, and no one would have wanted to kill Isaias (except his lunatic son-in-law Manasses who apparently *did* kill him), he was far too nice. The tradition that has it Isaias was butchered can only be true, one feels, if those who made an end of him had never known the man. A prophet, however downright in condemning wrong, who bears himself as modestly as does Isaias in the Fourth Book of Kings, cannot but be decently used; none of his ordinary hearers, surely, can we think of as treating him ill.

To return to the lesser prophet: 'They have coveted fields,' he says of the wealthy in Israel, 'and taken them by violence, and houses they have forcibly taken away; and [they have] oppressed a man and his house, a man and his inheritance. Therefore, thus saith the Lord,' etc. Of the evil prophets, making money and getting themselves fed out of their divine vocation, Micheas is more scathing still: 'if a man give not something into their mouth,' he says, thinking of the delicate fare he has seen at the refectory table, 'they prepare war against him . . . therefore shall night be to you instead of vision, and darkness instead of divination.' (Note here the similarity to Amos and Joel: 'darkness':—'night': negative evils—absence of what was theirs by right.) Of the unjust as a whole Micheas deplores that the 'best among them is as a brier, and he that is [considered] righteous is as the thorn of the hedge.' Micheas seems to have had occasion to witness clerical corruption at close quarters since he comes down to details in a way which is not repeated even in his treatment of the rich; thus from the laxity and license in Israel the prophet turns to Juda and tells how in Jerusalem, the Holy City itself, 'her priests have taught for hire, and her prophets divined for money' (another thought for those who are working and praying for the conversion of England, and teaching and directing souls within her shores) 'and they leaned upon the Lord, saying: Is not the Lord in the midst of us? No evil shall come upon us.' Osee, Amos, and Isaias are more or less summarized for us in the prophet's attack on the externalism and false confidence of the priests; this third chapter (returned to again in the sixth where he grieves over empty rites and lucrative sacrifices) is one of the gloomiest pages in Scripture, and it is only relieved by the promise contained in the fifth. It is with mournful reproach that Micheas looks at the ministers of a prosperous altar. Sermons to decaying religious have doubtless been preached from these chapters. We can imagine a de Rancé or a M. Olier taking down his Micheas for a text before facing a compulsory retreat or diocesan assembly. Micheas sees the tragedy of a cooling priesthood, and tries by warning, reproving, and inviting, to kindle again the spark that first responded to the love of God. It is not a relaxed observance that worries him, but a falling away that is inward . . . a spirit of compromise with this world, an un-living appreciation of the next.

ii

Having so far underlined the threatening aspect of the prophecy, it is time to assert quite definitely that dawn rather than doom is Micheas' prevalent *motif*. He looks further ahead than any of the Minor Prophets; the final restoration of the 'remnant' is seen by Micheas with a clarity of vision that others can show chiefly with respect to catastrophes resulting from a rejection of the Lord. The Prophecy of Micheas does not fall readily into groups according to subject-matter, so it is unwise to split it up artificially, but especially in chapters v and vii it will be seen that the hope of an ultimate blessing is uppermost in the prophet's mind.

Characteristically, the relief of both nations is heralded by a 'woe.' This rugged shepherd of the North and South is not the man to lullaby his flock: 'Now shalt thou be laid waste, O daughter of the robber; they have laid siege against us; with a rod they shall strike the cheek of the judge of Israel'; and then, when he has humbled Jerusalem (the 'daughter of the robber') and prophesied evil of Israel, 'Thou Bethlehem Ephrata' is his glorious announcement, '. . . a little one among the thousands of Juda, out of thee shall come forth unto me he that is to be the ruler in Israel; and his going forth is from the beginning, from the days of eternity.' This is more what we are looking for, a familiar word at last—'Christmas'—to soften the severity of the rest. How close is this to an even more familiar text: 'In the beginning was the Word ... the same was in the beginning with God ... in him was life ... and the Word was made flesh, and dwelt amongst us.' Or how close again to the message of the angel, where the One Who is to come is spoken of as reigning 'in the house of Jacob for ever, and of his kingdom there shall be no end.'[2] Far from being a forbidding prophet, Micheas, as Doctor of the Nativity, lacks nothing of his senior's tenderness. 'This man shall be our peace. . . .' 'I will wait for God my saviour . . .'' The calm of perfect trust is here, just as we meet it in the pages of Isaias, the stillness of the very early morning after the midnight storm. Waiting for the dawn . . . dark still, but 'He will judge my cause . . . he will bring me forth into the light and I shall behold his justice. . . .' And lastly, as the night begins to lift: 'He will turn again and have mercy on us . . . he will put away our iniquities . . . he will cast all our sins into the bottom of the sea.'

With this vast sunrise, then, in his mind, the rays of which are already edging the clouds with gold, it is not difficult to understand the contempt Micheas feels for the little selfish lip-service as he sees it going on around him, a travesty of the real thing. *That* will not hasten the dawn or atone for sin; but justice, mercy, a turning to the Lord on the part of priest and prince, purgation, labour . . . *then* would come forth 'he that is to be the ruler in Israel,' He whose beginning 'is from the days of eternity.' Amen.

[2] Luke i, 32, 33.

iii

Micheas, the man of the open, the provincial, the wanderer, is fond of mountains, and the hope he holds out of the Messias' reign is to be realized when the nations shall come in haste to 'the mountain of the Lord.' There on Mount Sion, God's judgement will take place. War shall be no more; the vine and the fig tree shall cover the husbandman, and 'there shall be none to make them afraid.' Micheas paints a delightful and now familiar picture of hardy warriors beating their spears into spades, and of plough-blades turning the soil that were fashioned for turning the flesh.

Peace, in Micheas, is no mere cessation from strife or the result of a successful foreign policy, for in that day 'we will walk in the name of the Lord our God.' . . . 'In that day, saith the Lord, I will gather up her that halteth, and her that I had cast out will I gather up . . . , I will make her that halted a remnant, and her that hath been afflicted a mighty nation . . . and the Lord will reign over them in Mount Sion, from this time now and for ever.' The peace of the Chosen People is certainly not to be the result of strategy: 'thou shalt come even to Babylon . . . there thou shalt be delivered; there the Lord will redeem thee out of the hand of thy enemies.'

Micheas is excused by both Archbishop Goodier and Fr. Hugh Pope for his lack of fire and imagery. Here is a passage which seems to me stirring enough; it is one of the prophet's appeals to Juda. 'Arise and tread,' Micheas calls out from one or other of his native hills about the Holy City—perhaps even Olivet itself—'arise and tread, O daughter of Sion, for I will make thy horn to be of iron and thy hoofs to be of brass; and thou shalt beat in pieces many peoples, and shalt immolate the spoils of them to the Lord, and their strength to the Lord of the whole earth.' True, Micheas has not the poetry of his herdsman brother Amos, or the throbbing tragedy of Osee, but his language is pure and strong and musical, more so than we should expect to hear from the lips of the Morasthite peasant.

After the eccentricities and contrarieties of Jonas it is perhaps fitting that we should be brought back again to the sterner type of prophet, the prophet of the old tradition who deals out punishments with a heavy hand and as readily lifts the repentant sinner to his feet. No better prophet could have been chosen for the purpose; Micheas would satisfy the most exacting. We picture the Morasthite as rather a remote, unlovely figure—like a Benedict Labre, only not so silent— passing backwards and forwards across the border, detested by the professional religious and feared by the aristocracy, a man with an intensely deep and entirely secret spiritual life. He makes friends only with the children on his many journeys, as rough men who are good sometimes can . . . perhaps it is because he tells them of a Fair Prince . . . Who is also a Fair Pauper . . . Who was not yet come, but Who would be of the stock of David . . . and would spring from the least among the thousands of Juda—from (and then in a whisper) —'Bethlehem Ephrata.' We picture Micheas at home only on the hills, where the winds would blow away the bitter images of what he had seen in the towns. A simple man with but one dream, the dream of a Messias. Amos, simple too, had many dreams and many ways of telling them. Micheas had but One.

WATCH AND PRAY

VII.   Nahum of the Single Thought

i

WITH close upon a hundred years between him and his predecessor, Nahum can be excused if he carries on the tradition not quite in the manner of the rest. He has got out of the stream, and must flow along a course of his own making. The great thing is that he is in the same direction and comes from the same spring; it is only a pity that in the rise of it he is himself almost completely submerged. One can but try, by peering into the flood and poking about in the rushes, to conjure up, however vaguely, an image of the prophet as he was.

At least we can be sure of one thing about him—his period. The Prophecy must have been written before the fall of Ninive (which is what the whole book is about) and after the fall of No-Ammon or Thebes. This gives a margin of sixty years: 666 to 6o6 B.C. The delivering of his melancholy message may have been occasioned either by the outbreak of hostilities on the part of Assyria (of which Ninive was the capital) or by the formation of a pact on the part of all Palestine defending itself against Assyrian aggression; provocation of some sort is suggested by the Prophecy, and it is also unlikely that so violent a diatribe as that which we meet in Nahum should have been hurled at a far away city in pursuit of the abstract theory that the infidel shall come to naught in the end. Nahum is both very sour and very sure about Assyria's doom, and one feels that as God had given him reason to be sure, so the Ninivites had given him reason to be sour; something seems to have roused the prophet considerably.

If the Prophecy can be placed without much difficulty, far otherwise is it the case with its author. We have to look very carefully indeed within these sixty years to find a trace of the man himself. 'The burden of Ninive. The book of the vision of Nahum the Elcesite . . .' That is all there is to tell, and however closely we examine the thirteen words, there is only a limited little that they can mean. 'Nahum' signifies 'consoler' (clearly a name chosen by people who had no presentiment of the kind of book the little boy would one day come to write); 'the Elcesite' indicates his birth-place, Elkosh, later 'Elcesi,' now 'Elkozah,' a tiny village in Galilee,[1] . . . and 'Ninive,' the place his vision showed him; for the rest we must read between the lines.

There is reason to believe that Nahum left Galilee to live in the South since the only deviation from the main theme— that of cursing Ninive—takes the form of an 'aside' to Juda, not to Galilee. But whether, at the time of his writing the Prophecy, he was dwelling among the ruins of what had been the Northern Kingdom or whether he was enjoying the hospitality of Juda, he certainly did not feel himself called upon to comment on the moral state of his brethren in either place.

[1] 'Another Elkosh is pointed out near Mossoul as the site, and it is remarkable that both the Prophets who directed their prophecies against Ninive should have graves assigned to them there. In the *Vitæ Prophetarum* of Pseudo-Epiphanius, Elkosh is assigned to the East of the Jordan, but there is reason for thinking that the true reading of the passage puts it on the west near Eleutheropolis. A Judean birth-place would perhaps better harmonize with the prophecy. The Galilean site, however, has an abundance of tradition in its favour, and Capharnaum, "Village of Nahum," is, after all, the most probable place of the Prophet's birth.' Pope, *Aids to the Bible*, O.T. p. 382.

Nahum has eyes for nothing save the atrocities of Ninive and the awful calamities it is bringing upon itself.

A word about Ninive before we look at what Nahum has in store for it. Its wealth was fabulous and its wickedness was a proverb; the power of Assyria had been a menace to Palestine for generations, and in the century we are considering the menace had taken shape in reality. Repeated invasions had harried the country, and Juda had been deprived of its king. By the time of Nahum's appearance Ninive's pride— justified in earlier years by splendid if unscrupulous triumphs —rested on a false sense of security. Incessant warfare, carried on by means of a man-power that was morally on the decline, had reduced Assyria's strength without reducing its assurance or its affluence. There is nothing that breeds pride, whether in a man or in a nation, so much as a consciousness of power. That the consciousness is not justified by the power is a detail that seldom carries weight with the person or nation concerned; pride, like love and religious obedience, is blind. Ninive, for half a century before it sank, was leaning on its oars—on its diamond sculls one might almost say. Jonas had preached penance nearly two hundred years before and had been entirely successful; the subsequent lapse, therefore, was all the more heinous since there could be no question of defending these particular heathens on the plea of invincible ignorance. On that occasion the king, the court, and the whole people had been turned from their evil way and for a time at least—for how long it was we do not know—had worshipped the God of Israel. Then, when things are at their worst again, comes Nahum with his 'burden.' The apostasy, pride, and cupidity of the wickedest town on earth must be avenged.

ii

The opening of Nahum's Prophecy is abrupt and unusual.
Where other prophets make use of the same jerky first verse
there is generally seen to be a reason for it; they either launch
straight out into what their 'burden' is, or else give us the
words of the Lord Himself. Not so Nahum; Nahum delivers
a homily first. This has possibly been accounted for by an
authority whom I have not read, so I shall only say here that
the detail of Nahum's exordium has not been very satisfactorily dealt with by those I have. Indeed with regard to the
whole of Nahum's book, as with regard to the man himself,
there seems to have been singularly little clearing up or
speculation on the part of critics. The suggestions that follow
are avowedly no more than guesses, and so are not of the
slightest value from the critical point of view, but where facts
and theories are wanting and there is nothing to pull down,
reasoned fancies may be enlisted in an attempt to reconstruct.
Nahum's ghost, then, as I see it, is like this (I shall give my
reasons—such as they are—in a moment): a courtier; a
product of Judean education and now in the suite of Juda's
king; but Israel born; he has travelled; he has fought; and he
has studied; in appearance there is nothing of the 'prophet'
about him; he is not associated with the priests particularly,
though he is often seen in the Temple; no one would call
him a *dévot*. The scandals of the court, as of the clergy, have
no great interest for Nahum even if they ever reach his ears;
his whole manner of address is other-worldly; he is a scholar,
a poet, a specialist, he has one interest—the Assyrian question. He moves about the palace as in a dream, thinking
about the past and occasionally—but in secret—receiving
messages from God about the future. For a soldier he is per-

haps too reserved, and for a prophet he is perhaps too soldierly; we cannot have it both ways. But Nahum is not wholly a recluse; whenever a guest of the king's arrives from the East, or better still an ambassador from Ninive, Nahum buttonholes him and speaks to him in his own tongue. Fellow-members of the king's household are for ever to be seen discussing with him the troubles of their own less tranquil lives.

In due course Nahum dies, and among his things (military equipment, parchments, curios, devotional objects, and a quantity of maps) are found the pages of his book, closely written sheets which reveal the unsuspected character of their author. He has been a prophet all along, an instrument of God, a visionary. The book—brief enough, alas—is published and achieves immediate recognition; it is welcomed on its literary merits and because of its strong anti-Assyrian sympathies. It is welcomed also—but only, one suspects, by the merest fraction of the king's subjects—on account of its ethical value. As material for propaganda the work is favoured from above, and before very long the Prophecy of Nahum the Elcesite is ranked among the classics, specifically *Juda's* classics, jealously guarded and on no account to be identified with anything that had emanated from Israel.[2] But now to substantiate this diaphanous Nahum.

[2] If it was Josias who was on the throne at the time of the Prophecy's appearance, there would have been no difficulty in getting it appreciated as coming from the finger of God; there would have been no foisting of a pamphlet upon his people for its propaganda value; Josias was a most admirable young man. If, however, Ammon happened to have been reigning at the time, or if the work appeared, as is just possible, in the middle years of Manasses' rule, then the accepting and promulgating of Divine Revelation would hardly have come from the highest motives. The Holy Spirit can as well make use of vested interests as any other for the furthering of Its designs . . . *spirat ubi vult.*

iii

We have already seen that Nahum's approach is different from that of the other prophets who have gone before him; he does not announce that 'the word of the Lord came to him saying: Arise and speak to these people, etc.,' or that 'the word of the Lord concerning Ninive was that . . .'; he does not mention the 'word of the Lord' at all, he merely says that he has had a vision. It is true that in the account of the vision the Lord is found to speak—and in terms of furious accusation—but one feels that it is primarily the idea of God's wrath that Nahum wishes to impress upon Ninive, rather than the words God uses to show that it is there.

The first twelve verses are taken up with general principles; Nahum is giving in an introduction the meat of his 'burden,' and all that follows is to serve as illustration. The Lord, he says, is a jealous God and must take revenge upon His enemies; this He has the power to do just as He has the power to melt the rocks that He has made. He can be merciful, however, to those who hope in Him . . . then why, O why, resist the strength of God? The rest of the book is an account of what Nahum has seen and heard regarding those who are perverse enough to resist the force of his doctrine. Ninive remains obstinate? Very well, its dissolution is inevitable, and, to descend to the particular from the general, the *manner* of the fall will be . . . thus and thus. I, the Elcesite, have seen it.

Both matter and manner, then, are different in Nahum from what we meet elsewhere; he is also alone on sundry other counts. Nowhere do we find him echoing the Psalms as do his predecessors, and there are few passages in his Prophecy that can be even remotely paralleled in any other.[3] This is all the more unexpected because in time Nahum comes towards the end of the list of prophets, and had every reason as well as every opportunity to draw from their writings.

Not only does Nahum appear to be unfamiliar with the records of Revelation—and this it is, in conjunction with the scantiness of his references to ceremonial worship, that makes one think he was not a priest—but he has very little to say about the poor; here is a departure indeed from the habit of his forefathers! the upper classes as such are passed over in silence; to an Amos or a Micheas, for example, the subject of an Assyrian city would have given scope for a spirited display of ire. Nahum launches, it is true, an attack upon the nobles, but only because they were at the same time chieftains who treated their prisoners in a barbarous way. As oppressors of the poor the leaders of Ninive earn no reproach from Nahum—that was a side of their life he had no occasion to notice—and as for Ninive's rich women (the 'fat kine' class of Amos's Prophecy) the Elcesite was not concerned with them at all. We have seen that the aristocracy of Juda also escaped Nahum's scourge. Now why was all this? May we not assume that it was probably because he was one of them? I am far from suggesting that the prophet was for hiding the defects of his own class; it is more to imply that the man was so removed from the worldliness of his surroundings that the scandals which were going on under the same roof never came

[3] An outstanding exception to this might be cited in the likeness of Nahum's 'Behold upon the mountains the feet of him that bringeth good tidings and that preacheth peace' to the 'Beautiful upon the mountains are the feet of him that bringeth good tidings and that preacheth peace' of Isaias. The way in which both prophets, however, have introduced the phrase suggests that they were doing so between inverted commas—that there was possibly some sort of 'household word' to do with 'mountains' and 'footsteps' and 'peace,' and consequently that neither prophet was making a reflexion of his own.

up for consideration; at all events not in the way that they would have done had he lived among those who were suffering their effects. The groanings under the yoke at home may well have gone unheeded—Nahum probably took the system very much for granted—it was the reports that reached him of Ninive that stung the prophet's soul. And these reports, incidentally, would nowhere be more discussed than at the palace. All the straws seem to be pointing to a Nahum who is clothed in the scarlet and ermine (or the equivalent) of the king's lieutenants, rather than to a hemp-clad Nahum, a Nahum of skins and hair.

Another thing: though the Prophecy is based on the idea of God's Justice finally triumphing over evil, there is in it curiously little of direct spirituality. May not the reason be that the writer was not strictly a very 'spiritual' person? Good, yes, and quite terribly in earnest, but not on the mystic level of, say, an Osee, an Amos, or a Joel. The Spirit breatheth where it listeth, and is it not at least conceivable that the Lord, in an age when prophets were scarce, seized upon this not very extraordinary soul, rare only for the fidelity with which it responded to the graces of its state, and caused to be written a vituperation rather than a lamentation, a pamphlet rather than a promise? Nahum's is not a helpful prophecy, nor one that suggests a groping after transcendentals; but then Nahum was never called upon to 'help' particularly, and still less were metaphysics required of him; he was a plain good man asked to live a plain good life and write a plain good Book. Which he did.

This brings us to a further suggestion, equally tentative and already hinted at above, that Nahum *wrote* his message to the erring race and did not speak it. From what has gone before it will be seen that this has been taken rather for granted, and if the process of piecing together has, up to date, appeared probable enough, then fresh discussion is redundant. Suffice to note here two points only: one, that Nahum's style is literary rather than rhetorical,[4] and secondly, there is no reason to suppose that the prophet ever visited Ninive.[5] From what little there is to go upon it would seem that Nahum's vocation was to stop in Palestine and write his vision as it came to him. That he had a facile gift for words can hardly be questioned, but that he spoke them, and spoke them in Assyria, is very unlikely indeed. The few expressions that apparently have an Assyrian smack about them can easily be accounted for: Nahum, well-educated and much travelled (if we think of him as accompanying the sovereign on his numerous campaigns), would have had at his command a smattering of Assyrian. To have been tolerably well versed in dialects and tongues would have been part of the stock-in-trade which no courtier-soldier-diplomat could have afforded to neglect. Nahum, whose specialty seems to have been literature—and specifically the literature of foreign politics—would probably have been fluent in Egyptian and Chaldean as well as in the more serviceable Assyrian. Nothing would have been more likely, therefore, than that he should, when speaking of Ninive to the people of Ninive, drop naturally into Ninive phraseology.

It may be asked why the prophet is made out to be one of the king's suite; why not a lawyer, a physician, or, more probable still, a chronicler or court librarian? Certainly it is impossible to prove either the man's profession or social level

---

[4] If the reader wisely shrinks from taking my word for it, he cannot do better than examine the text himself. One simple test to apply is that of standing in front of a looking-glass and declaiming Nahum's words.

[5] If he did, and if he brought his 'burden' with him, we may be fairly sure that he was not suffered to return and write it out.

from his writing, but so noticeable is the martial tone of the whole work that the inside knowledge of a soldier may legitimately be deduced. 'The shield of his mighty men is like fire, the men of the army are clad in scarlet, the reins of the chariot are flaming in the day of his preparation and the drivers are stupefied.' The man who wrote that verse was no lawyer or physician. 'They are in confusion in the ways, the chariots jostle one against another in the streets; their looks are like torches, like lightning running to and fro. He will muster up his valiant men, they shall stumble in their march . . .' One feels that the clash of swords and the thud of hoofs was not just something he had listened to on the king's birthday at a review. In the third chapter he breaks out again, and every word has the ring of battle about it. 'The noise of the whip, and the noise of the rattling of the wheels, and of the neighing horse, and of the running chariot, and the horsemen coming up . . . and of the shining sword, and of the glittering spear, and of a multitude slain, and of a grievous destruction; and there is no end of carcasses, and they shall fall down on their dead bodies.' The passage shows that whether Nahum was or was not a soldier he was quite distinctly an artist; his vision has given to him a composition that will never be forgotten. After the feverish scene of strife he sees the contrasted and still more impressive sight of rest. The flashing chariots and frenzied horses are waved into the background in order to make room for death. With Nahum's verse before us we seem to feel the ghastly hush that has settled on the field. No breath of wind to flick the shredded banners into life, and the last rays of light have ceased to dance upon the spears and helmets of the slain. If Nahum is giving us blood, for the moment he is checking the thunder, since the picture he paints is one of stillness, not of rage. We

see only a motionless heap of dead, a crossless Calvary against
the greying sky. Those bodies will rot—like man like horse—
'and it shall come to pass that everyone that shall see thee
shall flee away from thee and shall say: Ninive is laid waste.
Who shall bemoan thee?' The gilt on the chariot wheels will
be licked by desert rats, and lean-necked fowl will nest in
plates of brass.

Reminding us of another dirge, the *Dies Iræ*—where the
chant dies down to what we think must be the finish and
then starts up again with a last gasping summons of energy—
the Prophecy of Nahum blazes likewise into flame once more.
'Yet she also was removed,' says the prophet of the renegade
city, 'and was carried into captivity; her young children were
dashed to pieces at the top of every street; and they cast lots
upon her nobles, and all her great men were bound in fetters.'
The action of it is terrific—vivid, forceful, seemingly relent-
less: 'Therefore thou also shalt be made drunk and shalt be
despised; and thou shalt seek help from the enemy. All thy
strongholds shall be like fig-trees with their green figs: if they
shall be shaken they shall fall into the mouth of the eater.' And
the final wiping out is absolute, 'their place was not known
where they were.' Nahum does not spare Assyria! There is
not even the least hope that with sackcloth and ashes it might
be spared. The last taunt is hurled at Assyria's king in person. 'Thy shepherds have slumbered, O king of Assyria,' says
Nahum to a ruler who was himself somnolent enough, heavy
as he was with wine, 'thy princes shall be buried; thy people
are hid in the mountains and there is none to gather them
together.' Nahum is not afraid of lodging in the highest
quarter the only personal reflexion that his Prophecy contains. He is used to dealing with the great, and has doubtless
given advice to kings at home; that kings abroad should

fail to keep their houses in order was no surprise to him. One
only hopes that the devout little novice Josias was able to
benefit by Nahum's ripened views. But to the dissolute sovereign in his capital, the Elcesite is adamant: 'It is your fault,
O King,' says the enemy foreign secretary, 'too late now, but
your fault . . . the shepherds, your ministers, have idled away
their time and the flock has been dispersed,[6] to you it must
fall to weld the scattering nation into one, but other things
have claimed your time . . . "thou hast multiplied thy mer-
chandises above the stars of heaven" . . .'

And with that the parchment is rolled up and put away.
That Nahum's forecasts were fully and strictly carried into
effect we have it on the word of more than one pre-Christian
historian.[7] The year 606, at the latest, saw the fall of Ninive,
which came as the result of several combining causes. The
Medes, assisted by the Scythians and Babylonians, were at the
city gates; desertion from Ninive was wholesale; panic reigned
among the poorer classes while the nobles were drowning
dull care in liquor. The crisis came when the Tigris over-
flowed its banks and swept into the city over broken walls.
The king, in desperation and very drunk, set fire to his palace
and himself perished in the flames. It would be hard to imagine a more dismal *finale*. One looks in vain for the earthquake, but short of that the picture is complete. Ninive, like
the great Babylon of the Apocalypse, is finished. Amen to it.

Notice how clearly the prophet was allowed to see the end
—down to the details of a broken wall, a court debauch, a
fire, and a sudden inundation. These are particulars which,

[6] A further reason for the wane of Assyria's power besides that of the moral
decline may be seen in the system it employed of extensive deportations.
Besides weakening civilian life, it meant the packing of the army with mer-
cenaries or slaves or even prisoners of war.

[7] What follows in the way of particulars is taken mostly from the footnotes
of Farrar's *Minor Prophets,* pp. 148-151. It seems that Ktesias' account, preserved by Diodorus Siculus, is the main source of information.

had they not been verified to the letter, would have struck
the reader only as further indications of a poet's pictorial
skill. As a master of the lyric style Nahum deserves high
praise, but for prophetic material his inspiration ranks among
the very greatest; one only wishes he had written more about
the Lord who had wrought it in him so to prophesy. Having
brought us to our knees before the repaying Majesty of the
Lord we would willingly suffer ourselves to be taught by him
to raise our hands in supplication.

iv

And so the devout reader of the prophet Nahum may be
pardoned if he transports himself in spirit to the palace of
Ammon, king of Juda (or, a year or two later, to the court of
the boy-king, Josias) and looks down the line of ministers,
knights, and equerries, for a face to which he can put the
name of Nahum. Attention would eventually be drawn (so
the reader may go on to dream) to a deep-chested and somewhat ungainly figure, a Galilean by the build of him, but one
whose every movement had about it that much envied
'charisma' which men call breeding. There was Nahum, the
visitor would be told. A prophet, had it been asked? a seer?
One didn't know much about that . . . not as the rest of men,
decidedly, but 'prophet'? . . . possibly . . . it was only that the
idea of such a one in such a rôle was something new . . . as
good as gold, of course, and brave as the day was long . . .
but one had never thought of him as prophet . . . still, now
that one came to look at it, why not? But prophet or no
prophet, a great asset to the court was Nahum. And a poet
too, so they said, with all the nation's history at his fingers'
ends . . . a born pamphleteer if only he could be got to do
something in that way. It was believed that he *was*, as a fact,
composing some sort of open letter . . . but that probably

nothing much would come of it, one knew these soldiers with artistic temperaments!

And so it would have gone on. The visitor would then have watched the aged aristocrat take his leave, wondering at Nahum's early hour for bed. Was he not *too* aloof, perhaps, from these companionable Judeans? Certainly they were rather bucolic for the most part, but taken all in all, they were probably no worse than the majority of their kind.

Following Nahum to his bachelor suite we see him sink to his knees and pray. This customary act does not last many minutes, and though it is a prayer that absorbs the whole man, there is about it no sense of strain or violent tension. Once on his feet again, the prophet moves over to his table in the window; the 'open letter' would be resumed. His face would begin to glow and a great light would come up over his shoulders and shine upon the page beneath his hand . . . do we wonder that he cannot be busied with the life that is going on downstairs?

.   .   .   .   .   .

Ten years later and the same *cicerone* would be telling the same visitor that the gentle diplomat had died. How Nahum had gone up early one evening as was his custom and had not come down next day; and that those that had sought him in his room had been dazzled by the light that met them there. Yes, Nahum had been a prophet of the Lord—behold his 'burden' as a proof of it! Had one not suspected it all along? No? Well, if not a *prophet* in the strictest sense, one had always hailed him as a man of God. Yes, to be sure, he who had counselled kings had had for his counsellor the Lord. True indeed that the Spirit bloweth where it listeth and that often the Breath is hid and small.

VIII. *Habacuc: Doctor of Perseverance*

i

Assuming the tradition to be correct which identifies the Habacuc of the Prophecy with the Habacuc who appears—literally appears, and suddenly, though with every proof of his reality—in the Daniel story,[1] we have more to work upon than a mere shadow. Habacuc needs very little artificial reviving: he is as living a prophet as any (Jonas not excepted), and coming twice in the Bible as he does, with a wide gap of years in between, he provides the added interest of letting us trace his development and the effect of changes in fortune upon his *genre*. Were we not, however, to make the above assumption there would need to be some very special pleading indeed for the Habacuc who steps from the pages that follow, since given his Prophecy alone and no legend or Book of Daniel to back him up, there is little enough to be got of him from the text. Habacuc's 'oracle' is a tangle; as exalted a page of Scripture as one could wish to find, and for sheer spirituality perhaps as ambitious a work as that of any Minor Prophet. But nevertheless a tangle.[2]

[1] Dan. xiv, 32-39.
[2] It is only fair to say that Fr. Hugh Pope, the authority for most of these things, does *not* make the above assumption, in fact he draws the opposite conclusion. His reasons are given in *Aids to the Bible,* p. 384. The tradition, however, is so strong in favour that I feel no scruple in abiding by it, especially as the date question is not a serious obstacle once Fr. Pope's main argument—that the Chaldean menace was in its infancy at the time of the Prophecy —is seen to be open to doubt. This point will be discussed below.

If, accordingly, we first catalogue all extraneous pieces of information (Daniel connection, local legend, plausible deduction and whatnot), we can then proceed with the text on its own merits, returning at the end to compose a picture with the paints provided by both departments. This plan, with this prophet, would seem to be the most serviceable because then both kinds of reader can be catered for at once: the sceptic—not at all the kind of person I am writing for— can leave out everything except section iii and trust simply to the grace of God that he will see what Habacuc was aiming at, and the devout reader—the tender soul who yields to whatever information is forthcoming—he too is satisfied and can enjoy his Habacuc undisturbed.

Particulars, then, for Habacuc's biography amount to the following: born about 610 B.C.; a native of Bezocher; a priest; Juda the field of his prophetical labours; fled or was carried off to the neutral state of Ostracine during the Babylonian conquest; freed and taken back to Juda; took up farming; the Daniel incident; death about 520—after the Return—and tomb either at Keila (in Juda, about ten miles from Hebron), or at Chucoc (Nepthali), very much farther north.

Now as to how these details come, and whether any of them can be trusted.

First of all, Habacuc's dates as stated are approximately 610–520. We must put at least twenty-four years between the prophet's birth and the calamity he heralded, unless we make him leaning out of the schoolroom window to do so. If the destruction of Jerusalem took place in 586, Habacuc might still conceivably have been telling Juda to get ready for it in '88, aged twenty-two, but hardly much before. If, on the other hand, we give him a few more years and make him prophesy in full manhood, sav in the thirties, we are faced with two difficulties which are harder to brush away than the prophet's youthfulness. First, Habacuc's already long life can scarcely be stretched out so far as to include his seeing an end of the Exile, and second, if his birth is placed before about 625, one of the main assistances towards locating him at all is rendered valueless, namely, the absolute silence in Habacuc regarding idolatry. It is hardly believable, that is, that a prophet who was at the same time almost certainly a Levite, should have passed over a recognized evil such as idolatry when other less reputed prophets had but recently inveighed against it.[3] False worship is always a popular theme with the prophet, and the absence here is significant. The 'abominations' mentioned in Kings and objected to by the anonymous seers were not got rid of until Josias was of age, and up till then must infallibly have attracted the fire of any prophet worth his salt. We can only presume, therefore, that Habacuc arrived too late to see them; that is, after 630.[4] A further reason for placing the prophet almost under the cloud which he is waiting for is that he seems to be addressing the generation over whom he expects it to burst: '. . . for a work,' he says, 'is done in *your* days, which no man shall believe when it shall be told. For behold, I will raise up the Chaldeans, a bitter and swift nation, etc. . . .' Which, besides suggesting imminence, suggests also another difficulty: why if it was so close, was it so unexpected? This may perhaps be answered from the quoted words themselves—the Babylonians *were* a swift people. The storm cloud of Chaldean power did only, as a fact, roll towards Palestine at the last moment

---

[3] 4 Kings xxi, 10-16.

[4] Fr. Pope accounts for Habacuc's silence by saying that it was at the end of Juda's earlier reform that he appeared—when Manasses 'made good,' but this was nothing like as radical a reform as that of Josias some years later; and we need a radical reform to explain the silence.

before breaking. Nevertheless it is not easy to see how it came about that Juda was in ignorance of its near approach, and, if one may judge from the dominant note of the prophecy that follows—an appeal to take the present suffering with love—it must be admitted that the spiritual leaders of Juda, or at all events those who were leading spiritual lives were on the tip-toe of expectation, and had already tasted enough of pain to make them appreciative of the prophet's gospel. Leaving this particular aspect of the question in abeyance, we can still feel that we are not very far wrong in bringing the prophet into the world when the reign of Josias was drawing to a close. There is nothing to prevent him living on into the time when not only the land that had been Juda but all the known world besides was under the rule of the single king, Cyrus, Lord of ill-omened Babylonia.

The second of the statements made above regarding Habacuc's career—that he was a native of Bezocher or Beth-Zocher—is a legacy from the past for which it is impossible to find any foundation . . . other than that it *is* a legacy left over from the past.[5]

In support of Habacuc's priesthood, which is the next assertion, we seem to be on firmer ground again. One of the Septuagint manuscripts explicitly states at the head of the book in question that it is 'the prophecy of Habacuc, the son of Josue of the tribe of Levi,' and if this particular codex is insufficient witness, internal evidence would seem to settle the matter in the same direction. Never was a Prophecy so thick with psalmody, and the Psalms were then, as now, the prayer-book of the priest. In Chapter III alone there are eight

[5] The claim is mentioned by Farrar (op. cit., p. 173) and Bishop Challoner has thought it sufficiently well-authenticated to admit of its being printed without query at the head of the Prophecy of Habacuc as it appears in our Version.

parallels to the Psalter, and not only are the thoughts and words alike but the same musical directions appear to have been employed. If in a column of print from an unknown writer to the *Morning Post* (and Habacuc's third chapter would be rather less than that) were found three ideas of Shakespeare's, three from Sheridan, and two out of Bernard Shaw, the reader would legitimately conclude from allusions in the same article to 'amber floats,' 'wings,' and 'upstage,' that the writer was 'of the profession.' Habacuc's specialist knowledge, then, of the Psalter, together with his reference to the Temple and his mention of sacrifice, is considered sufficient to argue, if not to prove, that he was of the sacerdotal race. It has been thought by some who would go further—and heaven knows I can understand the desire to link up everybody in the Bible with everybody else as if they had lived in a Sussex village—that Habacuc was a disciple of Nahum's. But putting him where we have in the century this would hardly be possible; and besides, unless the foregoing sketch is very far from the truth, Habacuc would never have received his training—highly technical as we have seen it to have been—from so unpedagogical a master as Nahum. The only reason that seems to be advanced for the Nahum-Habacuc-chain-theory is that in every text Habacuc's book is the immediate successor of Nahum's. But, as Farrar points out, a better reason for the sequence may be seen in the fact that next after the deliverance from Ninive comes the equally important landmark in history, the tyranny of the Chaldeans.

One might further argue in defence of Habacuc's priesthood that the spiritual pre-eminence of his book is such that a careful and experimental study of sacred things must have gone to the making of it. But whether that study was the God-given business of the priest or the life-long inspiration of the layman it is of course impossible to determine from the text. As a final observation on this point, and only by way of forcing the 'argument from silence' into something like a roar, Habacuc has nothing to say against the clergy of his time. At first sight the omission might be put down to the writer's ignorance of clerical ways, and that consequently if we can be sure of one thing about Habacuc it is that he was not a priest. This kind of negative information, however, is usually —and here more charitably—taken to indicate the opposite, enabling us to conclude that Habacuc was a priest himself and that if anything *did* call for readjustment among the sacerdotal ranks, he, Habacuc, was loth to pursue the matter.

The fourth point, that the prophet's apostolate lay in Juda, can hardly be called in question because in the first place the Northern Kingdom had passed away, and in the second place because Chaldea is reproved for what it is to do to the Chosen People. Habacuc is not addressing himself to a pagan world; his psalms and hymns were understood in the land where he had learned them. None but men of Juda could have followed the drift of his book; none but men of Juda were left of the old tradition. No, certainly, it was Juda that had the full blast of the prophet's horn.

Moving on to the next assertion, it is possible that the legend making Habacuc leave his native land with the fall of Jerusalem takes its origin from not knowing what to do with him if he is allowed to stay. To let him remain on in Jerusalem when everyone else had gone creates the difficulty of having to account for the silence of a prophet who was eagerness itself for the furthering of the word of God. Ezechiel had been carried off to Babylon ten years before, and Daniel, hardly yet a full-grown prophet, was looking over his shoulder at the Holy City from along the same road; Jeremias had set his face towards Egypt and ultimately towards martyrdom . . . so if the desolation of Jerusalem is to be complete, then Habacuc must somehow be removed. There is no earthly reason, as a fact, to believe that he remained; we can even go one further and say that if he did he must certainly have been killed before long; the Chaldeans would have seen to that. We must remember that the Prophecy of Habacuc was both recent enough and topical enough to be of interest to others besides those to whom its spiritual message was directed, and hard words had been said of the invading sons of Babylon. So Habacuc journeys to Ostracine—St. Epiphanius is the authority for this—to enjoy another fifty years of life.

The Ostracine interlude is also insufficiently vouched for, and has so many variants, that we need not worry about it over much. Habacuc is depicted as fleeing to Ostracine, and then as fleeing from it; as being led in chains to Ostracine, and then as being released from it. The truth is that we have not the faintest idea how he got there nor how he got away. The solution lies buried in the sands of Ostracine. And possibly also in the tomb of St. Epiphanius. Content to leave it so, we can now pick up the threads again of Habacuc's life in Juda. Or rather we can splice the silken thread of his priestly life with the coarser twine of the life he was now to take up. Habacuc turns husbandman.

There would have been little demand in the Juda of this period for the services of the priest, and Habacuc would have been hard put to it to earn a living. He must have something besides his holy offices to provide even the most modest of revenues; he would devote himself to agriculture. A small farm could be picked up for a song in such spoliated land as Juda then was, and the price of labour would not be much more than one square meal a day and a roof to serve as cover for the night. And so we see a prophet of about sixty or sixty-five settling down, with a wealth of experience behind him, to the domesticated existence of the small landowner. We shall return to the farm period in a minute, as soon as the last of the legends has been buried along with the prophet whose name they enrich.

If I admit frankly that it is still a mystery to me how the tomb of Habacuc came to be associated with either Chucoc or Keila, we can dispose of the shredded list of biographical items and make our 'composition of person' straight away.

The 'composition of person,' then, amounts to this: A young Levite student, viewing the political situation with some alarm, doubles his prayers and penances against the coming storm. He is more longsighted than his fellow-priests and possibly more in earnest; he has nothing, however, with which to reproach his country-men, and social prejudices carry no weight with him at all. So far in fact is Habacuc from contemning his neighbour that if he fears for the nation's security he rests assured of the nation's spirituality. Now the Lord sees the uprightness of the prophet's heart and rewards him with a vision, showing to the bewildered, and on the face of it not very trusting, prophet that the Chaldeans are to be His instruments of correction, that they will in turn be overthrown, that the Chosen People must be taught to hope, and that the Just Judge will restore the balance in His good time.

The prophet[6] accordingly sets to work and either writes only or writes and preaches—but certainly *writes* (because the Lord has told him to)—the vision he has seen. Then, sudden and frightful, comes the first vindication of the prophet's forecast, Jerusalem's fall. The ink is hardly dry and

[6] Habacuc's prophetical status is unquestioned; twice in his own book and once in Daniel is he given his official title.

the dust has hardly settled before Habacuc is off and away
out of the country. Twenty . . . thirty . . . even perhaps forty
years go by. These are the blurred Ostracine years. Habacuc
is in Juda again, fixed in a course of charitable occupations.
So fixed in fact is Habacuc that not even the bidding of the
Lord to break his custom is well received. It is at this point
in our prophet's career that the Daniel account may be fittingly introduced. The passage as it stands in the younger
prophet is as follows:

'Now there was in Judea a prophet called Habacuc and
he had boiled a pottage, and had broken bread in a bowl;
and was going into the field to carry it to the reapers. And
the Angel of the Lord said to Habacuc: Carry the dinner
which thou hast into Babylon to Daniel who is in the
lions' den. And Habacuc said: Lord, I never saw Babylon,
nor do I know the den. And the Angel of the Lord took
him by the top of his head and carried him by the hair of
his head, and set him in Babylon over the den in the force
of his spirit. And Habacuc cried, saying: O Daniel, thou
servant of God, take the dinner that God hath sent thee.
And Daniel said: Thou hast remembered me, O God, and
thou hast not forsaken them that love thee. And Daniel
arose and ate. And the Angel of the Lord presently set
Habacuc again in his own place.'

Let us straightway admit that the Habacuc of this incident
is not the man we should have expected from what we know
of the man who wrote the Prophecy. He appears here simply
as a dear old gentleman, while the Prophecy that bears his
name would lead us to expect a sterner, deeper, surer personality. The homely figure with his porringer, garrulous and
somewhat wanting in the enterprise that makes for sainthood,

is a very toned down version of the daring questioner of the Lord whom we meet in the text of his own book. (Or rather—if we have not looked up the Prophecy for ourselves —whom we *shall* meet . . . in the sceptics' section, No. iii.) So strong, at first sight, is this impression of contrast that any attempt to reconcile the two seems nothing but a waste of time. On closer examination of the two texts, however, we can see the same tendencies asserting themselves, and the possibility is found to be by no means remote that the man who stands up and asks questions in the Prophecy, and the man who stands back and asks questions in Judea, are really one man after all. But as I say, this will be more clear when we come to deal with the delivering of the prophet's burden.

It is here that we pause for a moment, and lean upon a farmyard gate.

ii

Say you have traced the author of the Prophecy thus far: the fame of his genius has followed him from Juda to Ostracine, and from Ostracine back again to Juda, and men have pointed out to you the place where the saintly prophet lives. And say that before you beard the great one in his den you take out your copy of Daniel with you for a walk, and you read the fourteenth chapter several times.

In front of you, planted in a fold of Juda's hills, is a rather tumbledown little estate—a group of huts and barns bundled together anyhow within a crumbling wall; your eye turns naturally to the least mean of these abodes of man and beast, and you see a coil of smoke rising with the dignity of a lily into the cloudless blue. Somewhere there, you tell yourself, beneath that undistinguished roof, is writing or resting or praying the greatest living prophet of the Lord. You take the straw from your lips and you feel for your Old Testament and you ask yourself for the hundredth time: *Is* he the Habacuc of Daniel?

And say you push open the gate and step across the uneven square of yard . . . and say you look in at the window.

An old gentleman, very hot and dishevelled, is busy about his pots and pans. So busy is he in fact that you might stand at his elbow all day without attracting the least attention. Whatever he was in years gone by, he has certainly found himself now as a cook; he is obviously as happy as a schoolboy. Perhaps it is only the modelling of his hands that reveals a capacity for other things; surprisingly un-elaborate is his face, but it is not a common one; intense application has joined his brows in a permanent frown which removes nothing, however, from the merriness of the mouth. His short sturdy body suggests dynamic energy and brisk efficiency; you can see at once that if he were not at his kitchen range, this man would be mending a hurdle or propping up a trellis for his vines; equally well can you imagine him leaping over his hedges in the 'jubilus' of prayer, and, like St. Francis, dancing in the fields and crying 'Love.'

As you revise your picture of the quiet cell in which writes, rests, or prays the Minor Prophet Habacuc, a strong smell of spiced herbs floats out over your shoulders into the open air of Palestine. Dare you interrupt the prophet now with the question that is hanging on your lips? As you stand hesitating before what you suppose is the front door, you hear a shuffling of sandalled feet and the latch is jerked up beneath your hand. The door swings open on a single hinge and the owner of the establishment bustles out. He carries a tray of steaming bowls before him and nothing on earth can interrupt his purpose; he is past you before you have had time to ask your question; you have not had time to raise your hat.

With your eyes on the retreating figure you remember of course the reapers . . . you will be able to question them. You can see the men in the distance, white against the waving gold of corn, and as you gaze out into the glare from the shadow of Habacuc's porch you can hear, now a laugh, now a snatch of song . . . the breeze catches up the reapers' voices and adds, so it seems, a melancholy all its own. Nearer home, smooth honey-coloured oxen are treading out the grain. They snuffle and toss their blue-beaded headnets in the air. You hear the yoke creaking and the brasses jingling, and you thank the Lord that the diminutive driver is too idle to use his thong. Children, you remember, are chosen for this work in Palestine, not for their glibness but for their reticence; sullen infants trained in the school of taciturnity, one-syllable men they will grow up to be. You need not question *him*. Say you are lucky enough to find another soul within this place at such an hour, and say you approach him with your sentence ready framed, say you touch him on the shoulder, beginning: 'Sir, . . .' even then one doubts if you would get much more than points of general information about the master of the house: a better man to work for never lived . . . a great one with his books, so they said . . . and always running off on pious errands was the master . . . a little hasty, perhaps, when interfered with . . . good cook, too. . . .

You decide not to repeat your question. Or, better still, to overtake the man concerned and put it to him in person after all. There he is, mounting the slope of the opposite hill, not half a mile away. . . .

Hardly have you decided what to do with your problem when it is in a fair way of being solved for you. The prophet has vanished! You rub your eyes and look again, but there is nothing save the parted corn in the field and the smell of soup in the yard to show that there ever was a Habacuc at all. The sun beats down upon the cracked earth; the flies swarm about the piled up heaps of manure; the oxen show every sign of perseverance unto death. But Habacuc? not a hair of him. You think of the thirty-fifth verse of Daniel's last chapter, and you search the skies for an angel. Not a feather. Not a cloud. Not a movement, save where the blue meets the yellow of the horizon and there is a shimmering veil to soften the line between.

Can it be that Angels deal with Minor Prophets as suddenly as that? The business-like dispatch which was witnessed in the kitchen is nothing to the competence which cannot be witnessed in the open. No wonder Habacuc looked preoccupied a moment or two ago: he was evidently in converse with a messenger from God.

'And Daniel arose and ate. And the Angel of the Lord presently set Habacuc again in his own place.' Give it an hour all told. A strangely composed Habacuc is back in his kitchen. He is sitting on the spotless stone-flagged floor with the tray of empty dishes at his side and his legs stretched full length in front of him. His hands rest limply in his lap and he is in prayer. A smile appears on his bronzed face and spreads into a knowing, boyish grin; he opens his eyes—reluctantly enough it seems—and turns his head towards the window; he can just make out the reapers on the hill and can guess that they are not reaping any more; nor does he hear the sound of a laugh or the note of a song. They are sitting silent, he tells himself, and facing this way, with occasional glances at the progress of the sun. And no wonder! The prophet sighs and shakes himself. He looks at the platters as

if to make sure, and at the dirt that is clinging to his feet.
No, there has been no mistake; he has been in a den to-day
—with a very hungry servant of the Lord.

In five minutes the kitchen is a cloud of steam and pleasant
smells. Your question is answered—he *is*.

.   .   .   .   .   .

If we now go back and review the work that the prophet did
as a young man, we shall have more material for making a
character sketch as apart from merely fancying a picture.

iii

Like Nahum, Habacuc calls his Prophecy a 'burden,' which
is a term we are beginning to associate with—so to say—the
'bloodier' of the prophetical 'thunderings,' those messages
whose forecast of temporal calamity is less shot with rays of
hope. 'The word of the Lord' and 'the vision of So and So' introduce the text as a rule when the impending evils are con-
ditioned by the acceptance or non-acceptance of the threat.

The title, 'Doctor of Perseverance,' which I have ventured
to apply to Habacuc, has scarcely been borne out by what has
been said of him up to date; he has changed, according to me,
first his abode, then his manner of serving God, and finally
to a certain extent his character. It must be insisted, nevertheless, that perseverance is the key-note of his doctrine.
What consolation the prophet gives—and there is milk in
his words as well as blood—is based on a right understanding
of Eternity. If we are to bring order out of the chaos of our
lives, if we are to find happiness amid the miseries which
come to us from without, we must look upon time, says
Habacuc, as it is looked upon by God. Whatever be the
kickings on the part of man, the Lord at any rate is security

for everlasting; the fruits of men's labours and the temporal consequences of men's sins are alike swallowed up in the Immensity of God. 'Then shall his spirit be changed' is the prophet's sentence upon the worldling, the man who has only his twelve-hour butterfly life before his eyes, 'and he shall pass and fall; this is the strength of his god.' Straightway, bursting into praise of God, Habacuc goes on to give the sum of all his thought: 'Wast thou not from the beginning, O Lord my God my holy one, and we shall not die? Lord, thou hast appointed him for judgement, and made him strong for correction.' This idea of man's 'correction' as being the answer to man's pains (though the prophet seems to go back upon it a moment later, asking of the Lord an explanation *why*) is the truth that stands out clearest from the medley of his book. Through all the 'judgements' passed upon us we must hope . . . hope, not so much for deliverance—that may never come, either to ourselves or to the nation—but hope, quite simply *in* the Lord. It is a hope deferred, an invitation to endure for Him alone. We come into this world, we grope, we suffer, and we die. That is the sum. But we shall be miserable unless we grope and suffer right. The future is as much in the gift of God as is the past. Leave it so. It is the persevering in afflictions *now* that claims our care. If we look too long at what may lie ahead we shall fall away; if we look long enough at God we shall endure. Habacuc knows all this, and yet we find him crying still 'How long, O Lord . . . how long? . . . *Why* hast thou shown me iniquity and grievance? . . .' And even when he has been told the reason of it, and how it is that the wicked can be the instruments of God, 'Why,' he goes on asking, 'lookest thou upon them that do unjust things and holdest thy peace?' If Habacuc seems to question his own conviction, it is surely to give himself the excuse of hearing the Truth repeating it once more. It is often the case with active souls that they need time to make their offerings complete. It is not that they shrink, or doubt, or—deep down—even hesitate, they merely hold their breath where contemplatives breathe out easily whatever is in their hearts. With the contemplative there is nothing to block the passages between God and the soul, between the soul and the mind, and from the will back again to God. The assent may *seem* to the contemplative more grudging because his eyes are trained upon those very passages, and any counter-claim—'natural' obstruction—appears more hindering than it really is. All things being equal (which they very seldom are) and given fidelity in each to the light received from God, the active soul will take longer to respond; this is so even when in the natural order this active is as quick to make decisions as his contemplative counterpart is leisurely.

Habacuc, to return to him, was always one to rank objections high, but one feels that he would have been the first to subscribe to Newman's dictum that no amount of difficulties need constitute a doubt.

This prophet takes us, then, on to a remarkably high plane, and one which has not been dealt with in set terms by those who have gone before. Habacuc is the first exponent of the schoolmen's 'amor amicitiæ' as apart from 'amor concupiscentiæ'; he is the theologian who urges souls to the heights, rather than the seer whose warning is of what he sees in the depths.

The people of Juda, after the two purifications they had experienced in the one century—the first under Manasses, the second under Josias—were ripe now for Habacuc's appeal. Certainly they would never have responded to it earlier, and it is even doubtful if they did so now, but with such a preparation at the back of them they would hardly have missed its import. Habacuc was calling Juda, not to repentance but to perfection. Much the same call has been met with before in the Old Testament. To kiss the striking hand, to hope in God even though He exact the life He gives, etc., all this has been counselled by others; where Habacuc goes one further is that he makes the voluntary doing of God's Will the only means of finding happiness. Earthly success not only fails to secure real happiness but has nothing whatever to do with it. Failure is not sin and triumph is not virtue, both are the accidents of life, 'but the just man,' says Habacuc, 'shall live in his faith.' Fidelity, perseverance, unselfish love . . . these are life to the soul. It is a thought that is constantly before the mind of St. Paul—'the just man shall *live by* his faith.'[7] This Minor Prophet gives us Christianity though his Prophecy is not Messianic. How glad he would have been had he heard 'My peace I give unto you, not as the world giveth do I give unto you.'[8] Well, he knew that this peace was quite a different peace to that which the 'world' connected with the name. The peace that Christ and Habacuc would offer is peace in the show of wounds, and in the glad expectation of more wounds. 'Let us not leave the battle,' is the cry of an old Basque ballad, 'for the wounds we have received: those that are yet to come will make us forget the ones we suffer now.' But this must be said without a trace of bitterness, without a shadow of gloom. It is a peace which comes of apparently throwing away the very chances of peace; it is hope under a cloud, faith *in* a cloud; and love unfelt. 'Amen, amen, I say to you,' is the explanation, 'unless the grain of wheat falling to the ground die, itself remaineth alone, but if it die it bringeth forth much fruit. He that loveth his life shall lose it, and he that hateth

[7] Gal. iii, 11; Rom. i, 17; Heb. x, 38.   [8] John xiv, 27.

his life in this world keepeth it unto life eternal.'⁹ . . .'and I, if I be lifted up from the earth, will draw all things to myself.'¹⁰ Habacuc's Prophecy is nothing more than a commentary on these two texts; *'draw,'* notice, 'to myself,' and not 'compel'; Habacuc, like Our Lord after him, invites. Love attracts; and faith expresses that love which, when lifted up above the earth, fails to feel that it is being drawn.

Accordingly, if the message of Habacuc is 'to persevere under discipline, God dealeth with you as with his sons,'¹¹ it would be as well to look for a moment at the people to whom the exhortation is addressed. We have seen that the Chaldean bomb was about to burst, which must have meant that there were some at least in Juda to whom it was a menace at the time of his writing. We have seen also that never before had Juda been so free from blame. Commentators rightly see in these two facts the presentation of a problem which earlier prophets had not been called upon to face. It became the difficult duty of Habacuc to say to a righteous nation that the impending punishment which it did not now deserve must be borne for the sake of bearing it—and with no idea of its cessation. He does not point to past evils or future blessings, he merely tells them—as St. Paul is to tell their descendants—that they are to 'run by patience to the fight proposed,' and that the fight, incidentally, will be lost! The prophet must have had great confidence in his Juda, a confidence that subsequent fallings off under the Captivity might hardly seem to justify, and he must also have been leading a deeply spiritual life himself. A just man does not hold out to a nation an idea of blameless penance without an experimental knowledge of its value. It is further significant that for all his familiarity with antecedent Scripture, Habacuc refrains

⁹ John xii, 24, 25.   ¹⁰ John xii, 32.   ¹¹ Heb. xii, 7.

from appealing to precedent—the reason being, as Farrar suggests, that the example of individual sufferers would prove scant incentive when the soul of all Juda is addressed. 'No consolation save in God,' is the war-cry of the prophet Habacuc. A war-cry for a fated war.

Turning now to the text of the Prophecy itself, we can see from its structure how the theme we have been considering is worked out.

The first two chapters take the form of a dialogue between the writer and the Lord. This may or may not be a rhetorical device, but whatever it is it is very effective. The writer opens the discussion as we have already seen, by asking why all the wrong that he finds in the world is not once and for all put right, and the words he uses seem to suggest that he is thinking of Juda as enduring the evil from without only and not as contributing to it from within; it is the heathen neighbours with whom he is finding fault. The Lord replies to this by saying that redress will come in the shape of a tyrannous nation: 'I will raise up the Chaldeans . . . to possess the dwelling places that are not their own.' But what good will that do? Why should a foreigner be chosen to lord it over the Chosen People? Habacuc is determined to get the thing made clear: 'Why lookest thou upon them that do unjust things, and holdest thy peace?' and the prophet mounts his watchtower (Chap. II, v. 1) to await the Lord's answer to his question; it comes, and the manner of its coming as we picture it from this curious second chapter is dramatic. The young priest, eager and expectant, 'fixing his foot upon the tower'; and the Lord high up in the heavens preparing a vision for His servant. The lonely watching in the open air, with Naure enforcing lessons that are not learned over books of

theological training . . . the simplifying of Habacuc's soul
. . . the grace—new-found to Habacuc and almost sacra-
mental—of solitude . . . and then the sudden swooping down
of God, and the violent breaking of the prophet's silence.
'Write the vision,' cries the Lord, 'and make it plain upon
tables, that he that readeth may run over it . . . it shall surely
come and it shall not be slack.' There follow divine admoni-
tions: Juda must go on believing, go on trusting; Chaldea
will in due course ruin itself with its rapacity . . . 'but the
Lord is in his holy temple'—implying that all *Juda* has to do
is to keep vigil, even as Habacuc had done . . . for I, the Lord,
am her salvation.[12]

Here the dialogue ends, and the rest of the Prophecy is
devoted to a sort of pæan of praise; it is now that Habacuc's
grasp of melody and psaltery is shown to full advantage. As
it stands in the English the text is extremely hard to follow;
our minds are filled with a multiplicity of images, and not
until the last two verses are reached do we begin to see what
it has all been leading up to. But it is a glorious finish: 'I will

[12] This thought of finding happiness, 'salvation,' *in* God, as apart from what
He means to give us, is of the essence of Christian sanctity. The turning-point
in the lives of the saints seems to come when they leave even the heights
of seeing God in all things, for the still greater heights of seeing all things in
God. That this spiritual altruism results in the most intense happiness is
witnessed of course in the lives of individuals who have reached that stage,
but it is also vouched for—as in Habacuc—by God Himself. 'Those who have
no self-love,' in the words of a revelation granted by God to St. Mary Magdalen
of Pazzi, 'are those who have in all things renounced their own being and their
own will, in order to will and to seek My will alone. For, as they are altogether
emptied of themselves, they compel Me to fill them with Myself; and when I
communicate Myself in My fullness, I fill souls, and thus by grace they become
like to Me. Now you must know that when a soul is filled with Me, she no
longer feels suffering or toil because My presence strengthens her. She no
longer feels sadness, because I fill her with joy, in such a way that it may be
said that she has entered into the joy of her Master. On the other hand, the
soul that is not filled with Me is not fortified by Me either; and, as my
servant Augustine has said, she feels the weight of fatigue and weariness.'

rejoice in the Lord,' says the prophet with one eye on the
lean years before him, 'and I will joy in God my Saviour. The
Lord is my strength, and he will make my feet like the feet of
harts; and he the conqueror will lead me upon my high places
singing psalms.' There have been seventeen verses of melting
nations, crushed mountains, troubled tents, murmuring
oceans, fruitless vines, fallow lands, and every kind of 'rottenness entering into my bones and swarming under me,' and
now with the peroration we come out into the open again
and the gleaming light. 'I will rejoice *in the Lord*' . . . God *is*
salvation . . . the Lord alone is my strength. *He* is the conqueror, not I. His wins are in *His* good time, not mine. He
will lead me on to the hills, and my only business then will
be to sing.

iv

Considering that every prophet says much the same sort of
thing, it is astonishing to find a quality in each that marks its
possessor as unique. This is more than what is merely due to
characteristics of style, or to the nature of whatever occupation the prophet is following alongside of his prophetical
vocation. It is an empiricism of its own—a God-fostered way
of looking at things which is not quite shared by any of his
fellows.

The peculiar excellence of Habacuc could hardly be said
to rest in his strictly 'prophetical' powers; he predicts very
little that could not have been hazarded by any fairly en-
lightened thinker of his time. His writing does not suggest
that he was an orator, or even that he was anything very considerable as a writer. He is not a reformer, and he could not
be called a leader. Habacuc's distinctive eminence is due to
the grandeur of his doctrine alone.

There is no merit in blinding ourselves to the limitations of our heroes, and so it may be said without retracting one whit from our allegiance that Habacuc's style is not easy enough to make the reading of his book a leisurely delight, nor yet dynamic enough to carry one off on the wings of enthusiasm. The Prophecy of Habacuc is a 'penetrating study,' and while it shows the writer's insight into spiritual things, it reveals at the same time a particularly pleasing picture of contemporary Judaism—a picture the spirituality of which one would scarcely have thought to see. Short as it is, the book is a treatise rather than a tract, and the author is not so much the threatener of the old tradition as the theologian of the new. It must not be thought, however, because Habacuc is not a red-hot revivalist and because his Prophecy lacks lyricism, that there is an absence of freshness about the book; there is a certain amateurishness in Habacuc that is one of his major charms. In fact one might say that this immaturity of expression, when combined with his originality of thought, is yet another indication that Habacuc was a young man when the Lord revealed to him His word. Habacuc plays sundry variations on the one theme, and for this a master hand is needed if the thing is to be done comfortably. He very nearly succeeds; and where he fails, we feel it does not matter in the least. His gospel, not his skill, is what we want.

.   .   .   .   .   .

'*Habacuc,* the same as some think,' says Challoner in a note to verse 32 of Daniel xiv, 'whose prophecy is found among the lesser prophets; but others believe him to be different.'

So there one is.

IX. Sophonias the Mannered

i

WHEN it chances that a man is chosen by God to be at once a prophet and a prince, it is but fitting that we be made aware of it. Sophonias's foreword is Sophonias's pedigree. True, he only goes back four generations and so escapes the charge of snobbishness, but even then the genealogy includes a king. Justly proud of his ancestry, Sophonias is maddeningly humble about himself; there is no personal biography whatever. He gives us the reign in which he prophesied, and he leaves a few clues in his writing as to what kind of a man he must have been, but that is all.

> 'The word of the Lord that came to Sophonias the son of Chusi, the son of Godolias, the son of Amarias, the son of Ezechias, in the days of Josias the son of Ammon king of Juda.'

The name Sophonias signifies 'watchman of the Lord' or 'the Lord guardeth' or 'him whom Jehova hideth,' and one wonders why the experts make so much of Hebrew names, since they never seem of the smallest consequence.

The prophet says that he received the word in the days of King Josias; this being so it must have been in that king's earliest years of rule since idolatry is given as one of Juda's greater sins, while Josias, as we have seen, had removed the 'abominations' from the land before he was out of his teens. Sophonias was probably dead by the time that his longed-for reforms were undertaken, for we nowhere read of Josias consulting him though we know that the king was wont to seek guidance in matters ecclesiastical and spiritual.[1] It would have been all the more natural for Josias to turn to Sophonias had he been alive since the two were related to one another, sharing as they did the same great-grandfather. Jeremias was prophesying in Juda at about the time that Sophonias was at work, and there is every likelihood that the two prophets were on intimate terms; at all events they seem to have borrowed from each other's writings, though critics are in doubt for the most part as to which came first in the order of time. The parallel passages are not sufficiently telling to quote; the reader is asked to take them for granted and to pass on to the second verse:

> 'Gathering, I will gather together all things from off the face of the land, saith the Lord; I will gather man and beast, I will gather the birds of the air and the fishes of the sea, and the ungodly shall meet with ruin; and I will destroy men from off the face of the land, saith the Lord.'

From this brief reprobation, directed against all mankind, Sophonias plunges straightway into the message he has for Juda; he will return again to judge all nations presently. The *schema*, be it noted, in which the Chosen People are *first* dealt with, is new to us if we have followed the methods of the Minor Prophets up to date; the arrangement employed hitherto has been to start off by cursing the world in general and then to curse the Jewish world in particular. Sophonias, characteristically though quite unconsciously, adopts the opposite plan of the Major Prophets. He is the only Lesser Prophet to do this.

[1] 4 Kings xxii, 13.

'And I will stretch out my hand upon Juda, and upon all the inhabitants of Jerusalem; and I will destroy out of this place the remnant of Baal, and the names of the wardens of the temples with the priests.'

Sophonias can think of nothing worse, apparently, than that a man's name should cease to be! especially if he is so respectable a person as a 'warden.' The verse seems to conjure up a sort of Trollope situation, with a cathedral instead of a temple and black-coated deans in the place of the priests.

'And them that worship the host of heaven upon the tops of houses [will I destroy] and them that adore and swear by the Lord, and swear by Melchom.'

Idolatry in its various forms, from open worship of false gods to acts of superstition, seems to be the evil that most infuriates the prophet, and as always in the case of those who cry out against the evils of their time, it is idolatry at home that rankles, idolatry in a people schooled to worship the one true God. To whom much is given, of those much is expected, and they who swear by Melchom are the more to be punished if before they have sworn by the Lord. There is a special doom, then, for apostate Jews while the votaries of Baal will get it anyway.

ii

The skeleton of Sophonias's Prophecy is simplicity itself:
The 'Day of the Lord'—God's Anger and Judgement (Ch. I).
The Call to do Penance. (a) Unbelievers (Ch. II). (b) Believers (Ch. III; vv. 1-8).
The Promise of a Blessing (Ch. III, vv. 8-20).
The Prophecy contains three chapters only, eight verses

of which are devoted to benediction as against forty which are taken up with woes. When reading the Prophecy for the first time, the turn in the last chapter from doom to dawn is unexpectedly sudden, but one feels when getting to know the prophet better that this is just what Sophonias wanted it to be. To do him justice, Sophonias uses none of his literary devices for the purpose of attracting attention to himself, his only aim is to drive his message home. The result is that however polished his writing it is never precious, while on the other hand, however arresting it is as a pamphlet it can hardly be considered winning as a poem. He is a curious person, Sophonias, and for once we can form no kind of picture as to what the man was like; the most that can be said of him is that he was knowledgeable, cultured, observant of life around him, and possessed of no illusions whatever about his fellows. We imagine him perhaps as being chosen by God almost in spite of himself—much as we have imagined Nahum to have been chosen—not on account of his worthiness but rather on account of his position and because of his gift for words. (Aaron after all was chosen so—haphazard, it seems from the text[2]). Where we, with our limited vision, would be inclined to choose a more suitable man for the work of God, God Himself chooses the only one whom He wants to see doing it, and him He 'appoints that he should go and should bring forth fruit.'[3] For all we know, Sophonias may have been more interested in his family tree than in his 'remaining fruit,' but whether the prophet's aims were saintly or secular, he must have known very well that the power to prophesy the Word was an unmerited thing, the gratuitous gift of God. Indeed he says as much himself, 'He [the Lord] hath sanctified his guests.' As a fact, however, there is not the smallest call to belittle our prophet; he reveals a spiritual aptitude which

[2] Exod. iv, 14.   [3] John xv, 16.

must convince the severest of critics. In each member of the above three-boned skeleton there is a verse or two on which saints and sinners of every age might fittingly make meditation.

If the order in which the prophet's sentiments appear counts for anything, one may take it that superstition and hypocrisy are the irritants to which Sophonias feels most impelled to return. He ranks external ceremonial high (an 'offering' is one of the things he looks forward to in the ultimate restoration) but ritual worship only, lip-service—especially when allied to the lip-service of a pagan god—is detestable to him. All this has been the field of many a prophet's attack before now, and there are mournful witnesses from Saul and Solomon downwards to illustrate the theme, but one gets the impression that Sophonias more than most was the enemy of the hated vice. The prophets had no fears as to what the gods might do in answer to men's prayers, they feared what the prayers themselves would do in the souls of the men who prayed them. Faith cannot co-exist with fatalism, and it is to fatalism that superstition—to take only the least serious side of idol-worship —inevitably tends. It is this shabby compromise between the service of God and the service of Baal that fetches a prophet's scorn. Sophonias, were he living now, would probably have hard things to say of many who flaunt St. Christopher on their cars. (Not that St. Christopher should forthwith be unscrewed from the dashboard, but rather that some of the Christian virtues should accompany the Christian badge. People seem to forget that the first of St. Christopher's good qualities was his habit of giving lifts.) Our pious medals can become mascots and we can apply to our novenas the a-Catholic nature of a spell, but it means that our piety is degenerating into frivolity. We must not make pets of the saints of God. There are those who can be carried away with devotion to the Sacred Heart and yet to whom 'meekness,' 'pity,' 'penance' are things unknown and undesired. Sophonias would have been hard on these.

The prophet has a logical mind; he was first of all, as we have seen, against idolatry, taking in order the false worshipper (open idolater), the false priest, and the false layman. These, he says, have been turned from the true God by irreligion. Very good. But religion, he would have us know, is more than looking at the face of God with the eye of the mind, it is looking *for* God with the groping hands of faith. Sophonias blames 'Them that turn away from following after the Lord, and that have not sought the Lord nor searched after him.' His words are in the tradition; it is ceasing to *search* that constitutes the Jewish sin. We are not necessarily called upon to find, but whatever happens we must be discovered looking. 'Ask . . . see . . . knock;'[4] it is not enough to ask, says Christ, we must seek as well, and knock. 'Learn of Me because I am meek and humble of heart.'[5] Not 'look' at Me, or 'read' of Me, but *'learn'* of Me. . . . the test, Sophonias would insist, is simply that: do I want God? And just as the absence of the 'will to want' spells infidelity, so the presence of the 'will to want' means love. And thus it follows that the sadness which accompanies God's Absence is the truest sign that His Presence is being sought. 'Thou wouldst not search for Me,' said Our Lord to Pascal, 'if thou hadst not already found Me.' But we must go on searching all the same![6] 'Seek ye the Lord while he

---

[4] Matt. vii, 7.   [5] Matt. xi, 29.

[6] 'How do you expect people to seek you so much?' Mary Brotel (a nineteenth-century mystic, a servant who lived in Grenoble) asked Our Lord, 'You often make us seek You a very long time.' 'It is true,' was the answer, 'but that is what constitutes the merit of love. If they sought Me all their lives without finding Me, they would only have done their duty. I will take care that they are largely rewarded.' (From Saudreau, *Divine Communications,* Vol. II, p. 26.)

may be found, call upon him while he is near.'[7] 'Seek ye God and your soul shall live.'[8] And finally there is St. Paul in his famous Athens sermon: 'That they should seek God if haply they may feel after him or find him, although he be not far from every one of us.'[9] Like Sophonias in the passage we have just been considering, St. Paul has taken idolatry for the subject of his discourse. Look where you will in the Old Testament and in the New, it is always as a 'hidden God'[10] that you must search for Him. We are lucky if now we see Him in a glass, darkly, while we wait and watch—to see Him face to face. 'Blessed are they that have not seen and have believed.'[11] This must be our anchorage in the storm of faith. And even if we are not in danger of going down in the storm, there is always the ghastly boredom of the night. If the peril for most of us is in the darkness of hidden hope and unfelt charity, the words of Sophonias should teach us how to meet it. In the verse which follows what he has to say of seeking God—and surely this step-by-step advice is done deliberately —the prophet tells us how we are to make ready for the dawn. 'Be silent before the face of the Lord God; for the day of the Lord is near; for the Lord hath prepared a victim, he hath sanctified his guests.'

It is almost as if Sophonias were afraid that in our return to God we might hunger and thirst after justice too eagerly or break the darkened glass on which our faces press. We wait in prayer and not in a fever of anxiety; the lake must be still to catch the reflexion of the dawn. True, the 'day of the Lord' is a day of pain as well as a day of joy (for a price must needs be paid by the 'sanctified' of His 'guests'), but whether the 'day' is to mean suffering or happiness—or both —to those who wait for it, it is the *day of the Lord* and must

[7] Isa. lv. 6.　[8] Ps. lxviii, 33.　[9] Acts xvii, 27.　[10] Isa. xlv, 15.　[11] John xx, 29.

be waited for aright. 'Be silent,' says the prophet, yet how few there are that listen! Even in their prayer men shrink from silence, though the Son of Man was born in it.[12] Watching is made possible in silence; no need to tell the Lord we watch. We have Our Lord's advice on prayer, and still we fear and multiply our words. 'When you are praying, speak not much as do the heathens. For they think that in their much speaking they may be heard.'[13] It is not how much we say, nor what we say, that marks the value of our prayers, but what is said to us and whom we want to please in prayer. If we speak too fast we shall hardly have time to listen, and listening is indispensable to prayer. Yet we judge that our prayer has ceased when the flow of talk has ebbed away. Prayer is the 'raising of the heart and mind to God' and not the lips. Is 'saying our prayers' the only definition that we know of prayer? We do not talk of 'saying our conversation' when we go to see a friend. Be still, be still in prayer and see the coming of the Lord. On our side it is the steady gaze on God, the yielding of our soul to Him, the wordless absorption of the mind in Him, that constitutes our prayer; on His side, which is by far the more important side, it is the secret feeding of the soul with grace that is our prayer, and the strengthening of our powers in love.

In our concept of the perfect waiting for God's 'day'—the vigil kept by Mary for nine months—we do not somehow associate the time with speech. Would not Our Lady's own account have rather been 'Je le savoure'?—to quote what one of her twentieth-century children has described as his thanksgiving after Communion.

---

[12] 'While all things were in quiet silence, and the night was in the midst of her course, thy Almighty Word leaped down from heaven from thy royal throne . . .' (Wisd. xviii, 14, 15.)

[13] Matt. vi, 7.

When we turn from this to the more philosophical and psychological aspects of the prayer-problem, it is to the same conclusions that we are driven. 'When two things are to be joined making one,' says St. Bernard, 'the extremities of each must correspond,' and God, we know, is as a gentle air,[14] His breath is soft; the fire and whirlwind of our words to Him, even allowing that we can sometimes stir them up to this, are not as a rule of God. We are made in His Image, our prayer must accord with Him; we are made in His Image, the wax must be smooth to take It. If, moreover, our inward faculties are bound together in a single waiting upon God, it follows that argument, disturbance, din, must lessen with the purity of the prayer. It is a sign that the many parts of a piece of machinery are working well together when the reverberation-noises are reduced. The soul's longing after God, which in practice is hardly to be distinguished from the enjoyment of Him, must inevitably make for peace. It may, in the lower part of the soul—the 'sensitive' part—be perceived of as an ache, a painful thirsting after the Beloved, but it is a patient void rather than a restless suffering. The soul is content to sigh for God, and the reason for this is that God is already there and has given it the grace to sigh resigned. The powers of the soul are at rest, deep down, in their proper object—God. Since we have wandered so far from Sophonias already it may perhaps be pardonable to wander a little farther and to add that, because the whole being is occupied in this prayer which we have been considering, the body as well will share in its tranquillity; nerves are soothed and muscles relaxed, and we rise to our feet refreshed—as a man rises who has run and

[14] *The Lord is not in the earthquake. And after the earthquake a fire: the Lord is not in the fire; and after the fire a whistling of a gentle air* . . . (3 Kings xix, 11, 12).

slept. The exhaustion that sometimes follows 'successful' prayer is rather a proof of its imperfection than the reverse, showing that the emotions have had their way, and laying open the soul at the same time to possible reaction.

If prayer is not a mere arbitrary exercise but something absolutely vital to our souls, and if the whole condition of it is the laying bare of ourselves before the eyes of God, it is clear that any kind of artificiality *must* be wrong. And it is artificial to rouse up a fervour that is not there; the ecstasy of other people or of other times may not be suited to our present state. We can make use of fervours when they come, but provided we make not our liberty a cloak for sloth it is surely better to appear before the Lord as dumb. For most of us dumbness is the normal, and therefore for us it is the state most TRUE. God is truth. 'In the union of two,' remember, 'the ends must be agreed.'

But in effect what need have we of argument? We know the language of love when we see it, without listening for the syntax. We see a mother love her child. She speaks no word at all, she loves; she does not analyse her love, she loves. Nor, for the matter of that, does she analyse her baby or herself, she is far too occupied with love. In other words, she contemplates. And so with us; we gaze, to begin with, offering every particle of our being . . . and then, in the fulness of God's time, when He has judged the measure of our trust, he sends His Day, and the sanctities of God are understood.

iii

Sophonias's second chapter is almost entirely taken up with the judgement passed on the Nations round about. It is the least thrilling of the three divisions of his Prophecy, because after he has once repeated to the unworthy but still believing

Jews the already familiar injunction to seek, seek, seek (three times in the one verse), he draws up a list of the peoples under sentence. The fourteenth and fifteenth verses are more interesting but their similarity to Isaias is so marked that one shrinks from drawing conclusions about Sophonias. For instance, it might be urged that our prophet was an ardent nature-lover and that he had a particular flair for the pathetic situation, but as we know that Isaias was far more perceptive in these departments it is perhaps unwise to pronounce too definitely.

The verses in question run as follows:

> 'And flocks shall lie down in the midst thereof, all the beasts of the nations; and the bittern and the urchin shall lodge in the threshold thereof; the voice of the singing bird in the window, the raven on the upper post, for I will consume her strength. This is the glorious city that dwelt in security; that said in her heart: I am, and there is none beside me. How is she become a desert, a place for beasts to lie down in? Everyone that passeth by her shall hiss, and wag his hand.'

iv

The real Sophonias is revealed in his third chapter, where, steeped in the profoundest gloom himself, he all but drowns Jerusalem in a sea of woe. He seems to have reason for it. The Holy City is a 'provoking' place indeed, and the prophet is right when he deplores her lack of faith. See how she has refused the discipline of the Lord, and how, when He stood afar off, she failed to trust in Him, and when He drew nigh, disdained to win His love. 'Her princes,' so the reproach runs on, 'are in the midst of her as roaring lions; her judges are evening wolves, they left nothing for the morning.' What a picture of harshness and rapacity! and from the very quarter in which we look for dignity and calm. 'As sober as a judge' . . . as voracious more like.

'Her prophets are senseless men without faith; her priests have polluted the sanctuary; they have acted unjustly against the law.' The whole point of a prophet is his faith; and the priest is judged by the service of his altar; and the Law is alike the life of each. That the prophets are senseless is sad enough, but this may not be altogether their fault; that they are faithless is horrible. Has any prophet worthy of the name managed to do without faith? The proverbial persecution which attends his mission can only be met by a living faith. From Amos in the Old Testament to Stephen in the New, it is faith that has paved the way for hope. No love, no discipleship; no faith, no prophet. And the priests of Juda? 'Polluted the sanctuary' have the priests; their offerings have been mockeries, their altars a reproach. It is a miserable thing to watch an indifferent priest at his ceremonies, but here it is something worse than a flagging zeal that calls for the prophet's lament. This mention of a decadent clergy, taken together with the reference to priests in Chapter I, seems to show that Sophonias was not a Levite. The same way of arguing cannot lead us to believe that he was not a prophet because there is no denying Sophonias's gift. (It is, however, significant that he nowhere *calls* himself a 'prophet'—which had the connotation of professionalism—choosing rather to say quite simply that he had heard the Word of God.) We need not think of him as being eager to hold aloof, but it is quite clear that he does not wish to be associated with either priest or prophet or judge.

Then, when the prophet's voice has almost failed for want

of the breath to curse, the song is renewed and the splendour of the Lord proclaimed; let us mark the turn: 'I have destroyed the nations and their towers are beaten down; I have made their ways desert so that there is none that passeth by; their cities are desolate, there is not a man remaining, nor any inhabitant.' But because of the remnant the ashes shall give birth to the Phœnix; the way of the faithful few will become the way of the many, and the Lord will be invoked from the lands beyond the seas. 'Wherefore expect me, saith the Lord, in the day of my resurrection that is to come, for my judgment is to assemble the Gentiles and to gather the kingdoms . . . because then will I restore to the people a chosen lip that all may call upon the name of the Lord, and may serve Him with one shoulder.' There follows a perfect picture in a single verse: 'From beyond the rivers of Ethiopia shall my suppliants, the children of my dispersed people, bring me an offering.' If the Ethiopian is to change his skin abroad, the Jew at home will make his Israel worthy to receive him. 'The remnant of Israel shall do no iniquity, nor speak lies, nor shall a deceitful tongue be found in their mouth; for they shall feed and lie down, and there shall be none to make them afraid.' The promise is quite definitely Messianic though there is no mention of a Messias. 'The King of Israel, the Lord, is in the midst of thee; thou shalt fear evil no more.' 'The Lord thy God in the midst of thee is mighty; he will save; he will rejoice over thee with gladness, he will be SILENT in his love; he will be joyful over thee in praise.' So the prophet returns, as he nears the end, to the quietness and silence of God's Love.

We are surprised to find that familiar terms like 'peace,' 'salvation,' 'might,' and 'joy,' are used without reference to the Saviour's Name. As a fact this is not so curious as it might appear; the prophet is only being faithful to his habit; the Prophecy as a whole has been singularly indefinite as to the concrete particular. It is true that there was no vagueness about what nations were to be 'devoured' together with Jerusalem, but the invaders' names, it must be noted, are withheld. Perhaps Sophonias wished the universal character of his Prophecy to be one of its special notes, judging that the guilty nations—and more especially the guilty Jews—would keep longer out of mischief if they regarded themselves as being always liable to punishment and not merely under a single condemnation. What Sophonias wanted to stress was the *theory* of the thing: that transgression must inevitably mean redress of some kind, and that redress itself is demanded only with the overhead view of the salvation that is to follow. Sophonias is not a Micheas or a Malachias in his preaching of a millennium; where these two prophets seem to see Jesus and preach from their vision of Him to His Father's attributes, Sophonias appears rather to have the Justice and Mercy of God in mind, deducing general and inevitable laws from them. He is thus a colder prophet in many ways than his fellow Minor Prophets, though the light he sheds is anything but chill. Not glaring, perhaps, or even very compelling, is the torch that Sophonias holds aloft, but the glow that we get from him is generous enough. He can never quite forget that he is the cultured scribe, suave and gracious, and possibly on that account is he less prone to the enthusiasms that we find in Joel or Amos, for example. 'Sophonias the Sophisticated'? —not altogether; sophistication implies a superciliousness. The most that can be said is that he used a shade too naturally the wits that had been given him by God. And there is nothing very terrible in that. A happier title would be 'Sophonias the Seeker'—and better, perhaps, than 'Sophonias

the Stylist' or 'Mannered' as we have ventured to call him—
especially when we remember that 'Sophonias' means 'watchman of the Lord.'

So there is a significance after all in the meanings that are
found to proper names. With this particular prophet, certainly, the 'giving of a name' was no chance thing; from the
last two verses of his Book we can see what he thought of
proper names. Among the richest of Juda's future joys was
the promise of a name, lasting and recognized by all. 'I will
save her that halteth,' says the Lord, 'and I will gather her
that is cast out; I will get them praise and a *name* in all the
land where they had been put to confusion. At that time
when I will bring you, and at that time when I will gather
you, for I will give you a *name* and praise among all the
people of the earth, when I have brought back your captivity
before your eyes, saith the Lord.'

What's in a name, you ask? A deal of Royal Blood, says
Sophonias (son of Chusi, son of Godolias, son of Amarias,
son of Ezechias who was king over Juda when Osee was
reigning in Israel).

X. *Aggeus the Unemotional*

i

IT IS perhaps surprising to find in the middle of the grand romance which is the history of the Jewish Restoration a prophet whose dominant note is 'the-business-in-hand-and-no-heroics.' But before we examine the seer himself it will be necessary to get a general view of the conditions which prevailed at the time of his labours.

When we pick up the books of the Return, among which we can number the last three Prophecies of the Old Testament, we are conscious of again a new approach. It is in the circumstances and personalities of the time that the reason for this must be sought, because there is no appreciable change in the manner of expressing Inspiration. In an egoist age like our own when history is read, except by those who study it, largely for the pleasure of finding parallels to modern times or personal affairs, it is understandable if we catch ourselves likening the post-Exilic leaders to the pioneers of the Gothic Revival or to the champions of the Pre-Raphaelite Movement. There is the Pugin in Zorobabel as well as the spirit of the Lord, just as in the nineteenth-century architect there was the holy zeal of Aggeus, Zacharias, and Josue. For even the briefest glimpse at these Old Testament heroes we need to keep our fingers in the Bible in several places at once: the First Book of Esdras deserves a finger, and the accommodating reader would do well to keep Jeremias and Ezechiel within reach since they foreshadow what Esdras,

Aggeus, Nehemias, and Zacharias record; these—and, if you will, Malachias (whom some identify with Esdras)—are the moving spirits of the reform, and it is to them consequently that the Chosen People owed—under God—the Temple's rebuilding and the ultimate replacement of the exiled religion within the Holy City's walls. Aggeus, as a fact, is not so much a promoter of the movement as the messenger to its more hot-blooded leaders; it might seem that he is heading for Newcastle with his coals while he himself is chilly, but when we actually examine his load and mark its effect, we can both judge of the prophet's temperature and see what was God's purpose in the matter. The events leading up to Aggeus's announcements can be briefly summarized as follows:

When the Decree of Cyrus was issued in 538 B.C. allowing the Jews to make their way back to Palestine, there was considerable hesitation on the part of the newly emancipated to avail themselves of the permission; the lure of Babylon had bitten deep. Daniel had done his best to inspire enthusiasm for a restoration of the old religion in the place that the Lord and tradition had assigned to it, and sure enough a few of the more public-spirited had trickled back to Jerusalem and had started putting up an altar, but it was not until Aggeus appeared in the rôle of a prophet—and a few months after him Zacharias—that the undertaking showed any signs of being permanent. What had been going on in Jerusalem between the arrival of the first pilgrims and Aggeus's first word was this (1 Esdras i, iii, iv): Josue (or Jesus, high-priest of the time and son of Josedec) and Zorobabel (a prince, the son of Salathiel and one-time page and courtier in the train of Cyrus) had settled down, and caused some seven thousand disgruntled Jews to settle down, in Juda and Israel. Having

given their people six months' grace in which to take stock of
their surroundings, the two leaders had 'summoned all the
people as one man to Jerusalem.' An altar had been erected;
the morning and evening holocaust had been resumed; the
Feast of Tabernacles had been kept; the thing was on the way.

While all this was being rushed on 'the people of the land'
—Samaritans mostly—made objections, but the two pioneers
made light of them and continued to bring back the old
observance. Every day a new ceremony, every day a new feast.
'And they kept the duty of the day in its day; and afterwards
the continual holocaust, both on the new moons and on all
the solemnities of the Lord that were consecrated and on
all in which a free-will-offering was made to the Lord . . . but
the Temple of God was not yet founded.'[1] It is quite clear,
the reformers were enjoying themselves hugely. They were
rich (being Jews they had not spent seventy years in Babylon
for nothing) and they spent their money lavishly;[2] before
they had been back two years the Temple foundations were
being laid. That had been a great day, and Esdras who recorded it was most certainly present at the function: 'Then
Josue and his sons,' says the chronicler, 'and his brethren,
Cedmihel, and his sons, and the children of Juda, as one
man stood to hasten them that did the work in the Temple
of God . . . and when the masons laid the foundations of the
Temple of the Lord, the priests stood in their ornaments with
trumpets, and the Levites the sons of Asaph with cymbals,
to praise God by the hands of David, king of Israel. And they
sung together hymns and praise to the Lord, because He is
good and His mercy endureth for ever towards Israel. And all
the people shouted with a great shout, praising the Word, for
the foundations of the Temple of the Lord were laid.' But it

---

[1] 1 Esdras iii, 4, 5, 6.   [2] Ibid, iii, 7.

was not all jollification; there were some present, very, very aged they must have been, who felt sad in spite of everything. 'Many of the priests and Levites and the chief of the fathers and the ancients that had seen the former Temple, when they had the foundation of this Temple before their eyes, wept with a loud voice . . . so that one could not distinguish the voice of the shout of joy from the noise of the weeping of the people, for one with another the people shouted with a loud shout and the voice was heard afar off.'[3] Through all this third chapter of Esdras the force and businesslike method of God's two servants fairly sweeps us along—as it must have swept along the remnant resident population together with the men of the Return. Josue had his books of the Law, and Zorobabel had his personality, and between them they cleansed the Augean stable before the untended oxen were fully alive to what was going forward. To do even the most dispirited oxen justice they probably did not resent the changes themselves so much as fear the consequences of what was being introduced; the real obstructionists in the end were the cattle from the stables next door. But even if we take the resident Jews and look at them, it can have been no easy thing for men of settled habits to submit to the new régime. Not without reason could they regard the newcomers as foreign innovators: who were these people who quoted a tradition which no one knew very much about . . . and of which *they,* the ones who had remained in Jerusalem all along, might well be expected to be the legitimate custodians? Poor Zorobabel, he must have had plenty of verbal persecution to endure, and this, coming from his own people, would have cost him far more than any opposition which he met with from the Samaritans. 'All that will live godly in Christ

[3] Ibid., iii, 9-13.

Jesus shall suffer persecution,'[4] and Zorobabel has always been taken as a type of Christ, Prince and Restorer of a fallen race.

The upshot of it was that King Assuerus was appealed to by 'the people of the lands'; the incident is as typical as any in Scripture of the way in which human perversity will block for a time the work of God. The picture in Esdras is complete: Zorobabel working himself to the bone in the furtherance of the Right Thing; there come to him 'enemies of Juda and Benjamin' asking to be allowed to take part in the building of the Temple to the Lord; Zorobabel, certain only of his mission to put things right *within* and suspecting these men of Samaria, turns down the offer, 'then the people of the land hindered the hands of the people of Juda, and troubled them in building; and they hired counsellors against them to frustrate their design . . .' As a matter of fact Zorobabel had answered the petitioners very roughly.[5] The last eight months had told upon his nerves, and the man was worn out. His time had been fully occupied, preparing ceremonies and attending them, interviewing architects, engaging masons,[6] ordering timber from Libanus,[7] seeing to the chant and the dress and the furniture of the Temple service, assisting in person—and from what we know of the man, probably with some verve—at the building operations, and lastly, wearying himself in that most difficult of tasks, 'keeping the people together.' Zorobabel can be excused for being curt. King Assuerus, who was Cyrus's son and successor, and who is also referred to as Cambyses and Artaxerxes, was apparently not in a position to make the allowances which we have made above, with the result that 'the work of the house of the Lord in Jerusalem was interrupted, and ceased till the second

[4] 2 Tim. iii, 12.   [5] 1 Esdras iv, 3.   [6] iii, 7.   [7] iii, 7.

year of the reign of Darius, king of the Persians.'[8] Assuerus
is certainly to blame for going back on his father's decree, but
the man was afraid; he had been distinctly told by the
Samaritans that 'if this city be built, and the walls thereof
repaired, thou shalt have no possession on this side of the
river.'[9]

And Zorobabel? he had tried so hard! Too hard? Surely
not; it was right to have pressed the interests of the Lord,
but it must have been a dangerous moment all the same for
the soul of that prince when the order came to cease. Had the
Lord brought him thus far for nothing? Had it been a delu-
sion from the start? What would the faithful think? He, their
God-sent, much-vaunted leader, would be branded as a
common impostor, a reckless and selfish enthusiast, trading
on the patronage of a Lord who had lent no sanction to his
doings . . . and good Jewish coin had been wasted withal.

Our hearts melt for Zorobabel. He was not even a priest
with his daily sacrifice to fall back upon, he had nothing
but a far distant future to hope for . . . and in the meantime
a sheaf of architect's plans to stare him in the face. If one
dare hazard the temptations of the great, the urge must surely
have come to bluff it out. 'There are the loyal few,' he would
have told himself, 'who will follow me to the devil and
beyond; and to the devil I would never bid them come. Why
not fight it to a finish here and now? And build away against
whatever odds?' We can often argue ourselves into believing
that if a work is once good in itself it is always good to work
at it. Whether or not the devout servant of God was impelled
so to resist we do not know, but what is certain is that he
did not. And this is where Aggeus enters in.

Aggeus was sent by God to put heart into Zorobabel. Far

<hr/>

[8] iv, 24.   [9] 1 Esdras, iv, 16.

from disobeying the royal command it seems that Zorobabel's acceptance of God's Will in the matter had been, if anything, only too complete. So utterly had the prince effaced himself that the abandoned foundations were being regarded as a reproach rather than an inspiration, and the Chosen People had slid back with a sigh (not altogether unmixed with relief) to their ordinary occupations (which were making money), feeling that there was an end to it. It was for Aggeus to point out that what looked like a finish was in reality but a delay, and that it was high time something was done about it.

ii

'In the second year of Darius the king, in the sixth month, in the first day of the month, the word of the Lord came by the hand of Aggeus the prophet, to Zorobabel the son of Salathiel, governor of Juda, and to Jesus the son of Josedec the high priest, saying . . .'

Thus Aggeus puts himself at once in a category all his own by addressing himself to two people only and not to a nation or tribe; his is a very special message to a very special body, and applicable only to a very special occasion.[10] We have seen how general can be the prophets—witness Joel and Sophonias; we see now how a prophet can be raised up by God to cope with a particular situation and how he can be kept down to that situation with a strictness that precludes any rambling over other fields. Aggeus's Prophecy occupies thirty-eight verses in all and hardly a line of it is off the point. 'I'm not

[10] Once only is Aggeus told to speak to the people and then his tidings are contained in a single sentence, 'I am with you, saith the Lord.' In its context it is an important remark and deserves looking up, but we need always to remember when reading Aggeus that his vocation is to communicate intelligence to pastors rather than to their flocks, though oddly enough the information he gives affects the sheep more than the shepherds. Although his manner is downright, the method of Aggeus is indirect.

here to preach perfection,' Aggeus seems to say, 'I'm here to
tell you two souls (who probably know more about perfection
than I do) where the faithful are in danger of *missing* perfection. The work of God must be resumed, *see you to it.*'

If Darius had just begun to reign when Aggeus spoke the
Word, the date is fixed for us as 520.[11] Assuerus Cambyses had
died the year before, and it was he, it will be remembered,
to whom the Samaritans had appealed when Zorobabel had
sent them home in a state of pique. As this had taken place
'in the beginning of the reign'[12] we can assume that the
breaking off of building operations was followed by seven
or eight years in which nothing was done at all—time enough
for most men to regard the thing as a lost cause. No sooner
does the new king ascend the throne than the Lord uses him
for the furtherance of His work. To this Darius the First
made no objections whatever.

Nothing could be more exact, it may be noted, than the
introduction which Aggeus gives to his Prophecy: the year,
the month, and even the day are given—to show, presumably,
that the Lord's reproach was not unreasonable, grass *had*
been growing under their feet and over the pavement of
the Temple Court. 'Thus saith the Lord of Hosts, saying:
This people saith: The time is not yet come for building the
house of the Lord. And the word of the Lord came by the
hand of Aggeus the prophet, saying: Is it time for you to
dwell in ceiled houses, and this house lie desolate? And now
thus saith the Lord of hosts: Set your hearts to consider your
ways.'

So we in the twentieth century are doing nothing new, then,
when at the first rebuff we fob ourselves off with the excuse
that 'the time has not yet come for building.' Ready enough

[11] Darius the Great (Hystaspis).   [12] 1 Esdras iv, 6.

to see signs of God's Will when they point in the direction of our own, we tell ourselves—and other people—that we are but waiting for the day when the work of God may be resumed. In the meantime we hang up the hammock of God's Will and go to sleep in it; the tools, God's chosen instruments, are left to rust.

Josue and Zorobabel were right to obey the king's command to cease; the Jews likewise were right to obey; for all concerned it *was* the Will of God *then*. But it was wrong to go on saying that the time had not yet come to build. It had. It was only that the time had not yet come for putting on the roof. 'Give us this day our daily bread'; it need not always be the same bread, there can be one kind to-day and another to-morrow; and it may be very silly indeed to go on eating yesterday's. Doubtless the valiant Zorobabel and the saintly Josue knew this well and were meekly awaiting a sign. If they had been a little precipitate the first time, they would listen now for the signified Will of God. It came. In Aggeus's eighth verse it came, and was welcomed, one ventures to think, with a shout. 'Go up to the mountains, bring timber, and build the house; and it shall be acceptable to Me, and I shall be glorified, saith the Lord.' We can almost see Josue jumping out of his sandals with joy as he hears the news, and grasping the hands of Zorobabel in his: There is demonstrative congratulation on both sides. God has been good. (But Josue's jumping days would, I am afraid, have been well nigh over by this time; he was one of those who had left Jerusalem in chains at the time of the Captivity.) 'You have looked for more,' says the Lord in His reproach, 'and behold it became less. . . . Why, saith the Lord of hosts? because My house is desolate, and you make haste every man to his own house.' There is a sternness in the message, but the recipients take it in good part and find it stimulating rather than crushing; they will now be able to quote the Lord's intentions direct, instead of merely goading the Jews at the point of their own devotion. And how does the listless nation take the news? '. . . and all the remnant of the people hearkened to the voice of the Lord their God, and to the words of Aggeus the prophet, as the Lord their God sent him to them, and the people feared before the Lord.'

So it was a success. And as a matter of fact it was even more of a success than that, because the Lord was pleased with the fear they showed Him and sent His messenger to tell them so. (This is the verse referred to: 'I am with you, saith the Lord.') No need to waste time pining away with regrets when there is work to be done; a few tears, perhaps, to mix the mortar, but it would be a pity to flood the foundations.

This is the end of Aggeus's first mission. So fruitful was it that scarcely had three weeks elapsed since the first hearing of the Word, when moss was being torn from neglected walls, and lank-weeded sods were being tossed into carts that for seven years had been used for other things. In less than a month from the renascence Aggeus was getting his second Word from God, which meant for Zorobabel another third-party intelligence.

iii

The second Word began as follows:[13] 'Speak to Zorobabel the son of Salathiel the governor of Juda, and to Jesus

[13] Fr. Pope draws attention to the faulty chapter-division which makes for confusion when trying to follow the dates at which these words were spoken. The first verse of Chapter II refers to the last words of Chapter I. Even the expert Farrar has been misled by this, making Aggeus announce the second revelation on the seventh day of the Feast of Tabernacles, whereas there is no means of telling what day it was; that it was some time in October is as near as we can get (v. 2). And as a matter of fact it is exceedingly unlikely that

[Josue] the son of Josedec the high priest, and to the rest of the people, saying: Who is left among you that saw this house in its first glory? and how do you see it now? is it not in comparison to that as nothing in your eyes? Yet now take courage, O Zorobabel, saith the Lord, and take courage, O Jesus the son of Josedec the high priest, and take courage all ye people of the land, saith the Lord of hosts, and perform, for I am with you, saith the Lord of hosts.' We wonder at first why such a practically-minded man as Aggeus should be preaching a homily on fortitude when the purpose of his calling is to give instructions. On examination, however, this second Word, if not strictly a series of instructions, is an instruction nevertheless; an instruction 'to lift up the hands that hang down and the feeble knees . . .' It is, of course, as we shall see when we come to quote the rest of it, a Messianic instruction as well. 'If you compare this Temple with the one that Solomon built,' is the way in which the prophet drives his lesson home, 'you will be disappointed; but you are not to judge its glory by its ornament; as one material edifice succeeds another, the glory of the House of God must surely gain in majesty; besides which, and we are nearer now to Him Whose Coming will make of the earthly House the Church of God.' And then comes the trumpet-blast to herald Christ the King: 'Yet a little while, and I will move the heaven and the earth, and the sea and the dry land. And I will move all nations: AND THE DESIRED OF ALL NATIONS SHALL

Aggeus would have chosen a big feast on which to proclaim his news in public for the first time; his earliest mention of the Word would surely have been to the two whom it most concerned, and who, in the message, were mentioned by name. The public promulgation may have fallen upon a feast-day, but this would hardly have been the day on which it was received. With this in mind the reconstruction that follows may seem more justifiable than would at first appear.

COME; and I will fill his house with glory . . . saith the Lord of hosts.' O ye Jews, look beneath the surface! O ye Jews, rise above these earthly hopes. . . . 'Great shall be the glory of this last house, more than of the first . . . and in this place I will give peace . . . saith the Lord of hosts.'

iv

It is fairly clear that all four Words were handed on verbally by Aggeus and only written down later. They are much more in the style of addresses than treatises—scrappy, full of repetitions, and suggestive of the clipped diction of a busy man. Furthermore, the Lord is reported as bidding the prophet '*speak* to Zorobabel the son of Salathiel, etc.' It is not allowing too much to the imagination, then, if we think of Aggeus approaching a busy group of amateur builders and drawing two of them aside. Indeed Aggeus was in all probability himself engaged on the work, for we learn from Esdras that when they began to build again 'with them were the prophets of God helping'; Aggeus would have been just the man for some straightforward 'none-of-your-circus-tricks' piece of employment, roughing out a piece of stone, for example, or measuring the pillar-caps. The scene, as the three men draw away from it out of earshot, is a lively one: picks flashing dangerously in the sun, spades being jabbed into the baked earth (for the rains were late this year and there had been a drought earlier on; see Aggeus i, 10, 11), the contrast of vivid colours, the sound of shrill voices, the hammering, the creak and rumble of wheels over broken and stony ground. The prophet's interruption has caused some stir. It is remarked that he stumbles in his walk, that his face shines, that he appears unusually absorbed. Some new message from the Lord, that is it! How else account for so much eagerness? And there they are, the three of them: priest, prophet, prince, and deep in thought or prayer they seem to be.

Priest, Prophet, and Anointed King . . . in five hundred years He would come who would possess in Himself the character of each.

Aggeus is explaining the inwardness of the Temple-comparison. He has said what the Lord has bidden him say, and though he is a man of few words he feels bound to make things clear.[14] Not that there was any need for him to under-line the differences that existed between this and the previous Temple; his hearers would have been perfectly familiar, from 3 Kings and 2 Paralipomenon, with Solomon's architectural ventures. They had doubtless many a time contrasted their own unprofessional attempts with the perfect organization that had attended the original enterprise. We can imagine them shading their eyes in jest, looking for the 'seventy thousand men to carry burdens' and the 'eighty thousand to hew stones in the mountain,' and the 'three thousand overseers' with as many 'rulers.' Of Solomon's Temple it had been said that 'neither hammer nor axe nor any tool of iron was heard in the house when it was building.' Why, in the building of this one, you could hardly hear yourself speak.[15] No, there is no occasion to enlarge upon the contrast which is hinted at by the Lord. What Aggeus is saying to the two men, one at either side of him, as he begins to make slowly back to where the Jews are working, is surely something like this: 'You know these people well enough to see that a second spring, however

[14] 'It is, of course, inconceivable that we have in these written prophecies all that Aggeus said, and hence it is probable that the prophecy as it now stands, represents but the fragments of a continuous teaching.' (Pope, op. cit., 389.)

[15] See H. V. Morton's explanation of why this verse (3 Kings vi, 7) has its particular and very unexpected significance. (In the Steps of the Master, p. 65.)

well managed by yourselves, will never last. Jewish blood has been weakened by years of suppression. Hopes have been dashed too often. Not only give a lead—as you are doing—but give an inspiration, give them the Messias. Tell them that the DAY is not to be delayed for ever and that they, these very workmen here, are providing for that day, are labouring over a ground that shall one day be trod by Him who is "The Desired of All Nations" . . . and that "in this place," to quote the words of God Himself, "I will give peace, saith the Lord of hosts." ' If this last sentence had been the prophet's one sole contribution to the corpus of Holy Writ, Aggeus would have earned his place as a master. It is a bid for the interior blessings of God. It asks for a view which should be wholly supernatural, a faith which should be unsupported by statistics, a hope which casts no reflex glances at the past. Just for a moment Aggeus seems to appear as a desperate figure standing at a cross-roads . . . the spiritual or the material, which? 'For we look not at the things that are seen, but at the things that are not seen; for the things that are seen are temporal, but the things that are not seen are eternal.'[16] 'For we walk by faith and not by sight.'[17] He may raise his voice and wave his hands in the air, but he knows that the silly Jews are not understanding a word he says.

And so the three men of God rejoin their countrymen. Zorobabel, more used to the sceptre than the hod, stares vacantly at the section of wall for which he has made himself responsible (it is not getting on very fast, he will talk less in future and really make an effort to be competent). Josue, his priestly robes girt up, bends awkwardly over his spade, and

[16] 2 Cor, iv, 18.
[17] 2 Cor, v, 7.

though he feels stiffer and stiffer every evening, his work shows greater promise than his friend's. And Aggeus, what of him? He goes home early, I expect, to prepare the sermon he must shortly preach. To-morrow? The day after? Anyway, some time soon.

The sermon is delivered, the 'statement' is made as to the spirit in which these labours must be plied. Criticism is stifled for a day or two; jibes from alien lips are met with joy of heart; thoughts are turned to wondering what the Messias would be like . . . and then the cursing begins again, the old longings for Babylon, the petty quarrels, the suspicions, the shirkings of the more unpleasant tasks . . . and, on top of it all, the rains. Not only an annual wet season, but *hail* day after day, day after day.[18] Oh, yes, it was a little hard.

v

If the second revelation marks the highest pitch of Aggeus's prophetical song, the next canto is rather a confession of failure. This time two whole months have gone by without a word from God—it is as if the Lord will give His second message ample trial. December sees the breathing of His Spirit once again. He has seen how His children have already wearied and so provides a new incentive to the work; it is a less noble motive this time, and the revelation is accompanied with stern reproof. Consoling it is that these stamina-lacking, adynamic, flabby-livered builders are not rejected out of hand. It is the way of God to give another chance.

On this occasion it is quite possible that the whole band was addressed by the prophet direct (unless we take it that the injunction to 'ask the priests' implies the suggestion that

18 Aggeus ii, 18.

the Temple clergy were to be subjected to a kind of visitation first of all); the text seems to hint that the occasion of the pronouncement was a liturgical assembly within the Temple precincts.[19] At all events the burden of the message is perfectly clear and need not detain us long, though the way in which it is set forth is at first sight confusing. The passage has to do with various defilings and purifyings; the student who is as unfamiliar as I am with the details of Jewish custom, is likely enough to miss the import of the message by being impatient of its wording. Since the framework, however, is only incidental to the subject-matter, we may leave out the earlier verses of the revelation and proceed straight to where the people are told that their work up to now has profited them nothing. 'All that they have offered there shall be defiled.' 'I struck you with a blasting wind,' says the Lord two verses later, 'and all the works of your hand with the mildew and the hail, yet there was none among you that returned to Me.' The Word is depressing enough in all conscience, but it is only a corollary of the one that went before. 'If you keep to the course of trying to satisfy your consciences'—this is what it amounts to—'by a mere external obedience to God, if you judge that He thinks more of bricks and mortar than of the will to serve, then is your service vitiated and your masonry unclean.' Always the same doctrine: the inward to be sought that the outward may be blessed. 'And *that* is why,' continues the prophet, 'your labours have failed to prosper: scarcity at home and hail abroad, but from this day forward,[20] if you listen to me, blessings will attend the labours of your hands.' The third revelation, then, ends on a somewhat metallic note. The Chosen People are not invited any longer to serve for love—they no longer had it in them to do so—they are merely

[19] Ibid., 14, 15, 16.   [20] Aggeus ii, 19.

told that service *without* love is meaningless and that with it, *all* service, and especially such as is connected with the Temple, is liable to reward. This is admittedly not the loftiest line to take, because the implication is inevitably 'you will find that it pays if you do as you're told,' but it is going too far to say—as Farrar says—that Aggeus *appeals* to motives of expediency. The Dean is again hard on the prophet when he says that 'a commonplace people is hardly capable of listening to any except an ordinary prophet . . . '[21] (I confess I have yet to discover 'an ordinary prophet'), and lastly, in his summing up, that 'he seems to have been personally deficient in energy, and of such small significance that he has left hardly any traces of himself in the history and traditions of his people.'[22] Farrar has no great love for Aggeus the Prophet. I have. To me Aggeus is a creature of boundless energy and immense significance. His personality is only equalled by his self-effacing zeal. Look at the prophet, and tell me if you do not see another Moses. Like the patriarch, Aggeus has to deal with surly Jews; like the patriarch, he is let down by them; he scolds, he exhorts; his solace is in the Word of God itself; there is the same murmuring to contend with, and for much the same reason: Babylon in the place of Egypt, and a ruin in lieu of a wilderness. Like Moses, Aggeus knows well what it is that God wants, and, like Moses, he knows the limitations of God's People. For both these servants of God the temptation must have been the same: on the one hand to soften the doctrine, and on the other to cast overboard all hopes for God's Children and to live to God alone. Retiring and meek by nature, Moses and Aggeus accepted the horrid publicity of the work entrusted to them. No, Aggeus was not as some would have us see him, the

[21] Farrar, op. cit., p. 190.   [22] Ibid., p. 194.

dispirited doctor of a tag-end theme, indifferent to what his message would effect; much more surely was Aggeus the tried servant of God whose circumspect judgement led him to deliver his burden in just the manner suited to the need. That he was a man of few fancies is obvious from his words (and doubtless on account of this was he chosen by the Lord), but that the fire of the apostle was absent from his heart is impossible if we consider what he had to do—and did.

vi

It appears that on the evening of the day chosen for the public announcement, after the people had been harangued by the prophet, the Word again descended upon Aggeus and he was moved to speak a second time. This is the last of the prophet's utterances, and it is directed towards one man only, Zorobabel.

There is no Scriptural foundation for the fancy that follows, though something of the kind seems highly likely. We can assume at all events that if the prophet was not already stretched upon his tressel bed, reviewing the happenings of the day and waiting for the solaces of sleep, he was at his oratory in mental prayer. Of a sudden comes the Word of God and the prophet is on his feet without demur. He shuffles on his shoes, he smoothes his beard, he trims his outdoor lamp . . . but wait, there would be no need for a light to-night, there would be a moon: had not the Lord promised an end of the evil weather?[23] Why, it was mild already . . . the cloak could be left behind. Now, where would Zorobabel be at such an hour?

And we think of the old man, staff in hand and eyes cast

[23] Aggeus ii, 19.

down, threading his way through the narrow, busy, smelly Jerusalem streets to the modest palace of Zorobabel. The Holy City has shown as yet no signs of retiring for the night. This unmistakably prophetical personage, as recollected as a Poor Clare, causes a slight flutter in the booths and on the balconies. Always severe-looking, Aggeus is a familiar enough figure in the daytime, but there is something sinister as well as significant in his walking the streets at night. Arrived at the royal dwelling, the prophet is told that Zorobabel is not at home. Dear, dear, this was a pity. It would have been pleasant indeed to have spoken the Word in that quiet ar-caded court, where the moonlight fell in a thousand patches as it streamed through the lacework of vines. Aggeus was no romantic, but the merest clod would have fancied himself leaning against that well in the centre of the flagged pave-ment and speaking to a prince about the Love of God. And what a prince! Well, if he was out, he was out, but where was he likely to be? At Josue's? No, Josue would be in bed by this time, getting in all the sleep he could before an early rise; to-morrow, as Aggeus well knew, would see the aged priest first at the Temple as usual, opening the doors of the temporary House of God, the enclosure within the enclosure, and sighing for the day when he would be able to do the same service in the permanent building (it was a forlorn sigh as the aged priest well knew). Leave Josue—so Aggeus reflects—to his night's rest, dreaming of a glorious past and a still more glorious future.

And so with thoughts that circulate about the Temple and its liturgy, Aggeus turns his steps towards the sacred site. Aggeus is not the man to waste time in a moonlit courtyard; he knows that were he to sit down he would probably go to sleep. A little walk will do him good, and he can return again before the dawn. What unconscionably late hours these princes keep! With his ample garments gathered to the knee, Aggeus can be pictured as he tip-toes his way between the puddles of the recent rains. (What a year of it they have had, to be sure! Drought to begin with and now these floods and all . . . well, well, it will be different from now on . . . 'from this day I will bless you,' are the words the Lord has used.) The moon's reflexion in the cart-ruts, the glint on the face of a spade that should have been put away, the diamonds that shine at him from the long grass . . . the prosaic old prophet feels that this is something of an adventure and he views the scene as one who discovers a buried city. Not only does the place look quite different to him without the noise and movement and contrasting shades, but the people who have worked there only yesterday—who have groaned and shoved and spat —seem to visit the scene like kindly ghosts, silent and suave, and ready to obey. No longer does the prophet wish to scold, no longer is he tempted to make representations to the Lord, no longer does he mind the mud or feel the stones beneath his feet; the night and the Word he has received have wonderfully soothed the prophet of the Lord.

We like to think of Aggeus moving about the foundations without a sound, and lingering here and there to pray to God. He knows the plans of the Temple inside out, and can see to an inch where every sacred thing will stand. His longest halt is in the Holy Place. He has forgotten about Zorobabel by now, and even about the message that he bears; he is busied with Him from whom the Word has come. Perhaps Aggeus wakes to the cry of a startled bird, or perhaps his feet are brushed by a scuttling rat. Perhaps he thinks of bed and makes for home in the grey dawn . . . (with a wave of the hand to Josue who is coming up the hill) . . . perhaps—and having conceded so far to fancy we can walk with Aggeus one step further—perhaps, while the moon is still holding the landscape, and an hour or more before the most watchful cock need stir . . . *perhaps* only, Aggeus skirts the Sanctuary and comes upon the Court of the Priests. His eyes turn naturally to the great altar, the only really finished thing about the Temple and certainly the only thing to look at in the Court of the Priests. See, there is a shadow on its surface. Black against the paleness of the slab and open to the vault of heaven is the shadow of a man. A gaunt and irregular cross lies stark along the Altar of the Lord, and there upon the steps with arms outstretched stands Zorobabel, Juda's prince, in prayer.

vii

The Word of God as it reached Zorobabel was a word of comfort and ran as follows: 'I will move both heaven and earth. And I will overthrow the throne of kingdoms, and will destroy the strength of the kingdom of the Gentiles. And I will overthrow the chariot and him that rideth therein: and the horses and their riders shall come down, everyone by the sword of his brother. In that day, saith the Lord of hosts, I will take thee, O Zorobabel the son of Salathiel, My servant, saith the Lord, and will make thee as a signet, for I have chosen thee, saith the Lord of hosts.' With this the Prophecy ends.

What is said by the Lord to His prince is the sum of what He has already told His people: *I have chosen thee.* 'There is no escaping that,' says the Lord by the mouth of His prophet, 'you are My chosen ones, enriched by Me above all others, required beyond all others to render Me the service I deserve, and finally to be beyond all others blessed. *You are*

My choice. I call you to be My saints.' How many hear these
words and still hold back! Lord, teach us that sanctity is in
Thy gift—and, after we have yielded up ourselves, that Thou
indeed wilt 'give unto us the increase.'

'The reason why we love,' says St. Augustine commenting
on St. John (*Not as though we had loved God but because
He hath first loved us*), 'is that we are beloved, and surely that
we should love is God's gift. . . . Though we were the object
of His wrath, yet are we loved by Him.' Sanctity, then, as a
finished virtue, as also in its beginning stages, is nothing but
the magnet gift of God. 'I have chosen you, and have appointed you that you should go and should bring forth
fruit.'[24] He chooses, we respond. He 'draws all things to Himself.'[25] We let ourselves be drawn. He crowns. Think you that
we do the greater part? Think you that we play no part at all?
It is not that He does *more,* or we do *more,* but rather—and
again from St. Augustine—He does ALL and we do ALL. This
takes us as far as words can go.

'That you should bring forth fruit, and your fruit should
remain.'[26] Zorobabel brought forth fruit (the most perish-
able of which remained five hundred years—till Herod over-
laid it with another and a far more transitory store). Aggeus,
he too was fruitful in his work; which has 'remained'; a Lesser
Prophet with a little Book; but as great a task had he as
any man.

[24] John xv, 16.   [25] John xii, 32.   [26] John xv, 16.

XI. Zacharias of the Visions

i

ALONE among the Minor Prophets Zacharias seems to set no store by conciseness. The scarcity-value of Zacharias is low. He goes on and on and on. In spite of the length, however, there is not a dull verse in Zacharias, while the Messianic theme, which it is the whole purpose of the Prophecy to develop, is so exquisitely handled that one wonders why such a halo of silence surrounds this prophet's head. The average Christian knows little of his Zacharias. Perhaps one reason why intending writers have drawn back is because of the task which must present itself before long of deciding whether Zacharias was or was not the author of the last six chapters of the book which bears his name; and when that is settled, of further deciding—in the event of a negative conclusion—whether the three concluding chapters are the work of either prophet that has gone before. In other words, the intending writer on the life and work of Zacharias has to face the possibility of there being three Zachariases instead of one. An undertaking indeed for the stoutest heart. The arguments for and against a *dual* authorship (to begin with) are briefly set forth in Fr. Hugh Pope's 'Aids' already so often referred to, while the possibility of there being a third Zacharias is fully discussed in *Le Dictionnaire de la Bible*, Vol. IV, 2520-5, as well as in Farrar, Newcome, Hammond, Kidder, and—if one is interested in ingenious speculation—Flügge.[1] For our purposes it will be enough to treat the whole text as it appears in our Bible, assuming for the present that it comes from the facile pen of a single and very versatile prophet.

Biographical certainties amount only to the following: Zacharias received the Word for the first time two months after Aggeus had begun to preach. The period of Zacharias's activity as a prophet, however, lasted considerably longer than that of his contemporary. We know for certain—even leaving out the last six chapters—that Zacharias was prophesying in the fourth year of King Darius, two years after his first appearance. The purpose of the two contemporaries was the same: to stir up the listless Temple-builders. From Nehemias and Esdras the prophet can be traced to a priestly family and so it can be assumed that he too was almost certainly a priest. It would be rash all the same to identify him with 'the son of Barachias' who is mentioned in St. Matthew (xxiii, 35) as having been slain 'between the Temple and the Altar'; not even legend, much less tradition, assigns to Zacharias the palm of martyrdom. The name was a common one (meaning 'The Lord Remembers') and is found in half a dozen places in the Bible. The only other item with which we can swell the list of historical data—though even this cannot be called a 'biographical certainty'—is the coupling of Zacharias's and Aggeus's names in the joint authorship of four of the Psalms.[2] Thus the memoir-material at our disposal for the study of this prophet is seen to be inversely proportionate to the prophecy-material.

Coming at the same time and having to meet the same

---

[1] Judging by the footnotes of various authorities, a host of others have entered the lists at one time or another. Cheyne holds strong views, but I am unable to trace the work in which he expresses them.

[2] Ps. cxlv-cxlviii.

problem, it is natural that we should want to compare Zacharias with the subject of the foregoing sketch, and before even we touch upon his writing (or rather upon his little *feuilletons*), and since it is now no longer necessary to give the historical setting, it may be well to note immediately the several points of similarity and contrast.

Aggeus heard, Zacharias *saw,* the lesson of the Lord to the Chosen People.[3] Revelation came into Zacharias's life like so many flashes of lightning, and an angel was needed to tell him what the revelation was about. To Aggeus Revelation came in the form of words well weighed and self-explaining. The visions which fall within the compass of the first six chapters of Zacharias were granted to the prophet in the course of a single night; the span of Aggeus's career as a prophet was none too long as we have seen, but for sheer expedition Zacharias's circumstance would be hard to equal.[4] The visionary is far more obscure than God's messenger, and the reason for this is not hard to find: Zacharias had to transfer the things of sight into another medium, the medium of words, before he could express himself at all; while Aggeus had but to set the type afresh. Zacharias, therefore, is of necessity less restricted, he can express his message—indeed *must* do so—in an original form, moulded by his proper personality. Small wonder if he is the more enigmatic of the two. Like Aggeus he is patently saddened by the picture he sees of contemporary Judaism, but one feels about Zacharias that he had more to fall back upon in his life than had the dour ascetic with whom he worked. There is a lyrical quality—and more important, a spiritual richness—about the Prophecy of

[3] This is so of the most representative part of Zacharias, the first part, which alone is fully authenticated.

[4] Unless we include the sixteen revelations which were made to Dame Julian in the one night, fifteen of which occupying five hours.

Zacharias that puts the writer high above his post-Exilic fellows. Certainly it is so that in the order of literary merit he deserves a greater praise than does Aggeus, and one is inclined to think that in the spiritual order also—though such cross-comparisons lead one nowhere—Zacharias enjoyed a deeper peace. From what one can see he seems to have lived above the battle; less liable, was Zacharias, to be cast down by adverse hap. He had his priesthood, we must remember, he could always draw from that. Aggeus, alas, could not.

ii

If we take the first of the main divisions into which the Prophecy naturally falls: Chapters I-VIII, we find that the main purpose is to outline the future of God's People with reference to the Coming of the Messias. The theme is treated in the following way:

The establishing of Christ's City or Kingdom (First three visions, Ch. I, 7-11, 13).

The character and office of the Messias Himself (Two more visions, Ch. III and IV).

The nature and construction of His Church (The sixth and seventh visions, Ch. V and VI).

. . . . . .

lapse of two years

. . . . . .

A 'Word' (not a vision) in answer to a question regarding certain fasts (Ch. VII).

Another 'Word' urging trust in the Messianic hope (Ch. VIII).

The part played by the Angel during the night of the visions is vastly interesting and at the same time wholly new to
our study of the Minor Prophets. (Unless we except Habacuc's
angelic transporter.) The Angel is spoken of, not only as in-
terpreting the visions for the prophet, but as externally mani-
festing the authority of God Himself; he issues orders and
foretells the future. Tradition has it that the Angel in Zacharias is St. Michael.

The reader cannot do better than read this Apocalypse for
himself. Familiar expressions will be found—texts that have
stared at us from the Church's Liturgy—and these may reconcile us as we wander through the rest. The humble wayfarer
is apt to get lost in the thicket of myrtle and olive trees,[5] but
there is enough to warm his heart if he only look closer and
keep his patience. To use Zacharias's own expression there
are many 'good words, comfortable words'[6] on every page of
the Prophecy, in this as well as in the Ch. IX-XIV section;
and they are words, incidentally, which most of us fail to
associate with the Minor Prophet, so reminiscent are they of
the great Isaias.

'Turn to me, saith the Lord of hosts, and I will turn to
you.'[7] This, coming as it does in the Bible text so soon after
the closing words of Aggeus, looks almost as if it were intended as a corrective to a careless reading of the doctrine of
Abandonment. Where in the foregoing essay we saw that
God alone 'giveth the increase' and that none can *force* his
head into sanctity's crown, here we are reminded that we
must *turn* deliberately to Him. It is Sophonias's 'seek, seek,
seek' over again. God is waiting and inviting, but turn to
Him we must.

Certainly the Prophecy of Zacharias is not wanting in 'acts

[5] i, 10; iv, 11.   [6] i, 13.   [7] i, 3.

for mental prayer': 'And I will be to it [Jerusalem: the soul] saith the Lord, a wall of fire round about, and I will be in glory in the midst thereof. . . . Sing praise and rejoice, O daughter of Sion, for behold I will come and dwell in the midst of thee.'[8] Could anything be better suited to the moment of Communion, when, hedging us about as with a wall, He dwells in the midst of us to listen to our 'praise' and give us 'joy'?

'For behold I will bring the ORIENT My servant.'[9] And then if we turn to the second section of the Prophecy we find the same glad watchfulness. However many were the writers employed upon the work, it was seen to by the Lord that they had but one spirit. It was a spirit that saw deeply into both the joys and the sorrows that were to attend the Christ. 'Rejoice greatly, O daughter of Sion; shout for joy, O daughter of Jerusalem; *behold thy King* will come to thee, the just and saviour; he is poor and riding upon an ass.'[10] It is almost as if the prophet were granted a pre-vision of the Entry; how could he have been subsequently misread? 'Poor' and yet royal at the same time, 'riding upon an ass . . . and upon a colt the foal of an ass.' It seems so clear. Poverty and Kingship: Justice and Salvation . . . and Sion ready to shout with very joy.

Then there is the charming pastoral of the whistling Shepherd: 'And I will whistle for them and I will gather them together, because I have redeemed them; and I will multiply them as they were multiplied before . . .'[11] for the hireling shepherds had earned their Father's wrath.[12] From this to the Sacred Passion itself: 'And they weighed for my wages thirty pieces of silver . . . and I took the thirty pieces of silver and I cast them into the house of the Lord to the sanctuary.'[13] And lastly, with the same vision before him of the Man of Sorrows

[8] ii, 5, 10.   [9] iii, 8.   [10] ix, 9.   [11] x, 8.   [12] x, 2, 3.   [13] xi, 12, 13.

—this time on Calvary—'I will pour out upon the house of David,' says the prophet, speaking with the voice of God, 'and upon the inhabitants of Jerusalem the spirit of grace and of prayers; and *they shall look upon me whom they have pierced;* and they shall mourn for him as one mourneth for an only son, and they shall grieve over him as the manner is to grieve for the death of the first-born.[14] Enough, surely, to satisfy the most conscientious Scripture-searcher in his quest of thought for prayer.

Emphatically it is prayer-starvation that the world at large is suffering from, but even among those who pray there is often traceable a certain under-nourishment, a lassitude that is unhealthy, as distinct from the rest in God that is right. Turgid, liverish, flaccid mental prayer comes mostly of an undigested vocal prayer: the heaviness and melancholy that follows a surfeit. In short ejaculations drawn from Scripture —texts such as have been quoted here, and broken up into single sentences—the devout yet dispirited searcher can hardly fail to come upon the leaven that will raise his mental prayer.

iii

When the night of visions is over, and when Zacharias has crowned the high-priest Josue,[15] the record is a complete blank for two years; and then the Word—the spoken Revelation this time, as apart from what is seen—manifests itself once more. The way it came about was this: 'Sarasar and Rogommelech and the men that were with him, sent to the house of God to entreat the face of the Lord, to speak to the priests of the house of the Lord of hosts, and to the prophets, saying: Must I weep in the fifth month, or must I sanctify

[14] xii, 10.   [15] vi, 11.

myself as I have now done for many years?[16] Jerusalem is
clearly the place where such enquiries should be made; the
religious, prophets and priests, are just the people to settle
the matter in a moment. Take it to them. The point to be
decided is as to whether the fasts which had been assiduously
kept up during the Captivity need be practised any longer.
They had mostly been started to commemorate one or other
disaster connected with Jerusalem or the Temple, and now
that the situation had so much improved in Jerusalem, and
the Temple was in a fair way towards completion, it seemed
rather ridiculous to go on fasting. It was not as if these particular days (four in the year) had been commanded by the
Law, they had been entirely of their own making.

Zacharias is bidden 'Speak to all the people of the land and
to the priests, saying: When you fasted and mourned in the
fifth and the seventh month for these seventy years, did you
keep a fast unto me? And when you did eat and drink, did you
not eat for yourselves and drink for yourselves?' And Zacharias refuses to pronounce. He makes it very clear, however,
what he thinks: the kingdom of God is not in meat and drink;
about these ceremonial acts of supererogation it matters little
either way; the people had imposed the fasts upon themselves,
they could presumably dispense. (A bad enough use had been
made of these fasts while they had lasted.[17]) Let the people
themselves decide. . . . But should they want to know what
things it was that god regarded as of importance . . . 'thus
saith the Lord of hosts, saying: Judge ye true judgement, and

---

[16] It appears that the correct reading of this passage is 'they *of* the house of
God sent, etc.,' and since 'The House of God' is synonymous with the name
of the town of Bethel (the prophet Amos reminds us of that), it is from this
city, Bethel, that the deputation comes for the solution of its case of conscience.

[17] vii, 6.

show ye mercy and compassion every man to his brother. And oppress not the widow and the fatherless and the stranger and the poor. And let not a man devise evil in his heart against his brother.' Elementary Christianity in other words. 'Religion clean and undefiled before God and the Father is this: to visit the fatherless and widows in their tribulation, and to keep oneself unspotted from this world.'[18]

And how did they take it? Much in the way that we take it when we are told in the confessional that our penances savour of self-love.

'But they would not hearken, and they turned away the shoulder to depart, and they stopped their ears not to hear.' How very natural were these sons of David after all! 'And they made their heart as the adamant stone, lest they should hear the Law, and the words which the Lord of hosts sent in His spirit by the hand of His former prophets; so a great indignation came from the Lord of hosts.'

It is a revealing passage, this. The Jews of two years ago would not have bothered about getting a sanction to, or a dispensation from, their customary fasts; they would have done as they pleased. But having worked for God day in day out, and having leaned upon the words of two prophets, their hearts have grown stronger, and the grace of God has at last made a little headway in their souls. After two years of what was—if not a 'converted' life in the full sense—a considerably bettered life, they feel the need to put their religious practices on a proper footing: either get permission *never* to fast (and so save all this worry about whether one is committing sin by not fasting) or else fast regularly and under obedience (and at least have the knowledge that the blessing of God is upon the project).

[18] Jas. i, 27.

The same solution to much the same sort of problem is sought by most people who are beginning to set their feet upon the way; and who naturally want to see themselves doing it. We know that fasting and similar practices are connected with the 'way,' and we want to disabuse ourselves of any error on the subject. If we are in earnest we are probably far more anxious to fast than to obtain a dispensation. We like to know that we are well on the 'way.' 'This is the way' we repeat to ourselves, and others are told of what an excellent way it is. Then comes a Zacharias to us and says, with all authority and seriousness: 'It *is* a way, certainly, but only *a* way, and you have to tread it very carefully because it is meant especially for those who have walked on the other way first, or at all events who are prepared to walk on the other way always—the way which is meant to suit everyone without exception: the way of Justice and Charity and Truth. It doesn't look nearly so attractive but it's the only way on to the way of penance, and if you follow it for any length of time you will find that it infallibly leads to what you are now asking for.'

'And it came to pass that as he spoke'—to return to the words of the prophet—'they heard not; so shall they cry and I will not hear, saith the Lord of hosts.' Probably it is because the Way is meant for all that it is so little prized. We despise common ground however green the grass that grows thereon. But our refusals will cost us dear; our fretfulness and pique can be more than an obstacle to perfection. If we spurn the 'weightier things of the Law' we may have to hear what was said of the Jews in the verse that follows the words last quoted: 'And I dispersed them throughout all kingdoms which they know not; and the land was left desolate behind them, so that no man passed through or returned; and they changed the delightful land into a wilderness.' There are few things more sad than the decay of something that was grand; it is like the estrangement of friends or the memory of peace in one who has lost it.

'When you fasted and mourned . . . did you keep a fast unto Me?' . . . 'judge ye true judgement, show mercy and compassion . . . ' It is not that we should avoid fasting (heaven forbid) or even that we should give up seeking occasions of fasting voluntarily, but only that we should avoid turning our backs upon what God manifestly values more.

· · · · · · ·

A second address, this time unprovoked by any deputation, closes the first part of the Prophecy; it is mostly an exhortation, as was its predecessor, to truthfulness, justice, and charity. It occupies one chapter and need not concern us here.

iv

The second section, Chapter IX to the end, is clearly very different from what has gone before. Even in the English it can be seen that the style is not the same, while it appears that linguistic differences exist as well. Historical allusions and the mention of idolatry as an existing evil, when we have reason to believe that the Captivity had cured the Jews of false worship, incline to the possibility that there is another Zacharias at work. The last six chapters may be divided thus:

The Triumph of Jerusalem over the Nations (IX, X).

The Apostasy of Present and Unworthy Leaders (XI).

The Relief and Subsequent Purification of Jerusalem (XII, XIII).

The Messianic Peace and Universal Recognition of the Lord which is to follow the Destruction of Jerusalem's Unfaithful Children (XIV).

The possibility already alluded to of there being yet a third Zacharias is suggested by the new tone which Chapters XII-XIV introduce. Both the attitude of mind in which these chapters were written and the moral conditions which the writer seems called upon to face are enough, so the experts tell us, to warrant the existence of an altogether new and original prophet. We leave him to them. What with the multiplicity of argument and the multiplication of prophet the Prophecy of Zacharias is a tangle. But it is a very inviting tangle to anyone who finds an appeal in reading detective stories, untying bits of string, snubbing textual critics, and skating on thin ice. It is the thin ice that precludes speculation here.

v

Through the mist that is his Prophecy we can but vaguely make out Zacharias the visionary. There may be two other Zachariases with him; there may be one; he may be alone. His head is carried high and he is seeing things that are not ordinarily shown to man. He bears the proud marks of violence in his flesh;[19] it has been his lot to suffer shame as well as pain (hired was Zacharias at the wage of a slave for the gifts that had been given him by God[20]). In teaching to an obstinate race the verities of God, his highest pitch of ecstasy is reached, not, as we should expect, when visions are pouring in upon him out of heaven, but when he speaks of the meek coming of Christ. On the Messianic theme Zacharias has a sureness of touch that can dispense with angels and images. Chapters IX-XI attain to a level which, one had thought, the literature of Juda's most flourishing period alone could scale. The post-Exilic prophet is a matter-of-fact person as a rule, and Zacharias of the 'middle section' is found to be astonish-

[19] xii, 10.   [20] xi, 13.

ingly alive. While retaining a fund of common sense—witness his treatment of the fasters—his soul-spurrings are as vivid and ardent as those of the most full-blooded Spanish mystic. We feel that while Zacharias is touching the realities of his life high up in the clouds that must always envelop him, enough of the man can be defined to be of practical help to souls. If for most of the time he is pointing up the mountain to show only that the summit is really there, it would indeed be foolishness on our part were we to follow with our eyes and ears alone.

XII. *Malachias: The Mystic*

i

LITTLE as it is intended, one can only suppose that the title of
this study will cause trouble. Every few years there seems to
be a fresh outbreak of interest in mysticism, and learned
authorities are found to vie with one another in telling us
What Mysticism Is. Their dissertations are sometimes spiritual and sometimes witty, but the question remains still
unsettled in the minds of most. Far be it from the nature of
a humble little book of this sort to make so bold as to enter
the lists; the great must grapple with the great. It is unbe-
coming on the part of a biography to wear the garments of a
pandect, and definitions, therefore, regarding Mysticism and
its ramifications will be carefully avoided. All that is claimed
in these pages is that the writer knows a mystic when he sees
one; and he seems to see a mystic in Malachias. The prophet
has, in other words, that which is found in those who are
recognized as mystics all the world over—St. Francis, St.
Catherine, St. Teresa, and the rest; and which we can call
the *mystic point of view.*

People are either in the Mystic Way or they are not. You
cannot be a mystic one day and back again a stockbroker the
next; though of course there is nothing to prevent you from
being a mystic and a stockbroker at the same time.[1] Mystic
experience may come in flashes but the *mystic life* is a 'habit':

[1] Except possibly stockbroking.

that is to say it really is a life.[2] And just as an artist is always
an artist though he be not a very good one, so a mystic is
still a mystic though he be a false one (or a true but not a
very good one). Once granted to a man the mystic point of
view, the world is a very different place from what it was
before or from what it is to other people. The difference between the ordinary man and the ordinary mystic is surely
somewhere here: where we at best re-act to creatures *as*
creatures—isolated instances of God's creative act—the mystic sees the whole scheme of creation. I do not mean that he
apprehends the universe in a glance (in some such way as it
was granted to St. Benedict, for example, to see the whole
cosmos at once—this was something directly miraculous), but
merely that he sees how God and nature and art and people
are capable of a single meaning. It is no longer: God in
heaven—we on earth. But rather: heaven, earth, we—in God.

The induction upon the Mystic Way—if one may rever-
ently posit a 'process' in a matter where any set method can
hardly be thought of—is normally something like this: first
of all the soul stretches out to God, willing and desiring all
that speaks to him of God (both what he sees now to be God's
Will and what may later on be sent to him beyond his recognition of it as God's Will): he removes, one by one, the obstacles that lie in the way between him and God; all that is
less than God he accepts but does not move a finger to obtain.
And this is as far as the beginner can go. There follows a
period when it seems to the soul that there is nothing whatever going on. The length of this depends entirely upon God
who measures the strength of the soul against the purgation

[2] Which is not at all the impression which one gets from the very interesting
and learned writings of Professor Allison Peers. His chapter on Francisco de
Osuna in *Studies of The Spanish Mystics* seems almost to take the opposite
for granted.

necessary, taking into account such things as habits of sin contracted in the past, works for which the soul is being fitted for the future, and the particular circumstances which surround the individual. Thus a man's occupation, health, retirement of life, opportunity for prayer, etc., will influence—though not necessarily determine—the time or the degree, or both, of the soul's painful non-doing. This period is called the Night. All this time the soul is haunted by the thought that its progress is being arrested. It wants to do more but it feels that there is nothing to be done. Which is perfectly true. What is being done is being done for it: by God. Far from arriving at an *impasse,* the soul is secretly forging ahead, or rather being forged ahead by the power of the Holy Spirit; it is being purified, refined, prepared, to meet what is in store. The next stage (and again it must be insisted that the progress does not admit of movements) is when God takes the place of all that has occupied the soul before. This happens in such different ways with different souls, both in regard to the manner in which it happens as in regard to what happens when it does, that no account of it will be attempted here. Nor, for our present purposes, need we discuss whether the whole preparation for the Way can be confined to the Night of the Senses or whether the Night of the Soul must also be passed before the person concerned can be accounted 'mystic.' Suffice to say that when God *has* flooded the soul with His light and taken possession, the soul is conscious of it and knows, for a time at least—though not a very long time—that life can never be quite the same again. There follows then a curious phase, and one which causes some misgiving on occasions to those who are watching the progress of the neophyte and who have not fully understood the designs of God, when the 'creatures,' the same rejected and then forgotten creatures, are gradually sent back again by God. The soul is sometimes a little apprehensive at first, fearing its own unruly affections of long ago, but soon it sees that instead of distracting from the sense of God's presence they seem if anything to minister to it. They have taken their place in the altered vision of the new-born mystic: God is between to shelter the soul from harm. To take a simile: a boatman pushes off a little from the shore (for just as far as the rope that is tied to a stake on the beach will let him); a mist comes up between him and the dry land; he sees less and less of the familiar objects ashore; finally he sees nothing but the mist, and this wholly envelops him. Then, when it has served its purpose, the mist begins to lift, and the familiar objects ashore are seen again, very dimly at first and then more clearly, but always IN the mist. For the mist (in this parable) never wholly melts. In some such way are creatures seen in God. Before, in the Purgative Way, the soul strove—with conscious effort—to see God everywhere, in each of His external expressions; it vested every beautiful object of God's creation with a little separate halo of mist all its own. Now, in the Mystic Way, creatures are still so many utterances of God but they are heard in one sentence, seen on a single plane with God himself.

For the consolation of those who are shocked by the apparent starkness of the mystic's renunciation and subsequent acceptance of creatures 'on another plane' and 'with a veil between,' a further word may be added. It is this: the lovely things of life are no less tenderly loved by the mystic than they were before; if anything they are loved more tenderly because they are more fully understood. Less selfishly are they loved, but not less loved. We shrink from the mystic's approach because we hate to think of yielding *anything* of our love, even the part of it that lies wholly in the senses. 'Let that go,' we say, 'and it will be a cold affair indeed: appreciation, perhaps, but not *love*.' We have need to grasp the fact that the mystic is not the man who is allowed to look at life only through frosted glass, but rather he is one of the few who are allowed to look at it through the eyes of God. *God's* love for creatures is no colder because unshot with concupiscence. The mystic's love of people, places, things, is but a pale—ever so pale—reflexion of that Love Divine.[3] The meaning of creation *is* Love. 'Wouldst thou witten thy Lord's meaning in this thing?' is Christ's way of explaining it to Dame Julian, a mystic if ever there was one, 'Wit it well: Love was His meaning,' and again, 'and so all things hath the being by the love of God.'[4] The mystic sees this more clearly than his fellow-men. His sight is more true, not less. His love is more true, not less. Thus it is of course that the miraculous is seen by the mystic as something ordinary; the supernatural is to him the natural, the everyday. It is no more surprising to him that the human body should rise in the air in an ecstasy than fall to the ground in a fit; to him there is evidently a very good reason

[3] How else can be explained the very real love that certain of the saints quite undoubtedly had for the things which of themselves were not of God? They loved because God let them love and because the creatures that they loved never for a moment interfered with the love of God. 'Who then shall separate us from the love of Christ? shall tribulation? or distress? or famine? . . . nor height, nor depth, nor any other creature shall be able to separate us from the love of God . . .' (Rom. viii, 35, 39). Take St. Francis with his love of nature, St. John Bosco and the enjoyment he obviously derived from his work among boys, St. Ulrich with his dish of venison . . . does not the secret of their pleasure lie in the fact that they found these things in God? and, having found them, that they held them always with a loose hand, ready at any moment to lay them down a second time? (Even since beginning this note it has of course occurred to me that two out of the three saints just mentioned—chosen absolutely at random—were, as a fact, required to yield up what they held: St. Francis went blind, and St. Ulrich's venison was turned into a cod.)

[4] *Revelations of Divine Love,* Chapters lxxxvi and v. And also: 'For soothly I saw that our Substance is in God.' (lviii).

for the levitation, or it would not have happened. But that it should not or could not have happened, it never enters his head to suspect.

Thus it follows that the doctrine does not confine itself to the lovable works of God's creation, but has its bearing also upon the problem of human evils. The accidents of life are seen as accidents no longer. Pain, misunderstandings, partings, death, waste—the whole gamut of human misery—all are seen related to the good in the loving economy of God. Suffering and joy are taken equally. They are of one piece. The coat is without seam. It is sin alone that clashes with the harmonious utterance of God.

Of God meanwhile the soul's conceptions tend to become more formless. The mist that was God and that came for a while between the boat and the shore is scarcely seen; it has entered into the soul itself.

I leave it to the reader to judge whether Malachias is one of the kind described or not. An occasional phrase from his Prophecy may stand out in the reading of it to confirm the surmise which is proffered here. It would take us too far from Malachias were we to prolong the discussion further and to ask whether all the prophets were mystics or only one or two. The verses to examine are these:

'Have we not all one father? hath not one God created us?'[5]

' . . . the wife of thy youth whom thou hast despised . . . did not One make her? and she is the residue of his Spirit? And what doth one seek but the seed of God? Keep then thy spirit and despise not the wife of thy youth.'[6]

' . . . and presently the Lord whom you seek shall come . . . and he shall sit refining and cleansing the silver, and he shall

[5] ii, 10.　　　　[6] ii, 14, 15.

purify the sons of Levi, and shall refine them as gold and as silver, and they shall offer sacrifices to the Lord.'[7]

And there are others. Malachias who sees things as they are in the sight of God is for ever helping us to peer through the veil on which their shadows fall. *We* see but the shapes of things while the mystic sees their reason and their place. 'For the lips of the priest shall keep knowledge,' says Malachias, 'because he is the Angel of the Lord of hosts.'[8] Yes, the priest is a man, we know that; but much more is he the familiar of the Lord and the keeper of God's Truth. 'Look for God's Messenger, O ye people: regard thyself as such, O thou priest.'

ii

Practically all the information regarding Malachias—what there is of it—is given for us in the little paragraph which Bishop Challoner has placed at the head of the Prophecy. 'Malachias' means 'Angel of the Lord.'[9] He is believed to have been a priest, though there is nothing in his Prophecy to show for certain that this was so; the tradition, however, is certainly strong, and the prophet is found to return with insistence to the subject of the exalted state of the priesthood and to the present deplorable falling short on the part of its members. Malachias's constantly reiterated preoccupation about the sacrifice confirms the supposition. It is clear that the Prophecy was written long after the Exile had come to an

---

[7] iii, 1, 3.   [8] ii, 7.

[9] 'Malachi' is considered more correct, meaning 'My Angel'; it is possible that the word is not a proper name at all but merely what has come down to us as a name from some such title-phrase as 'The Word of the Lord by the Angel' or 'As it came by His Angel.' The author of this Prophecy is not mentioned by name anywhere else in the Bible; which is surprising since he is believed to have been a contemporary of the chroniclers Esdras and Nehemias. Indeed the name, whether in connexion with the Prophecy or not, occurs nowhere else in Scripture.

end, probably in the fifth century B.C. and some eighty or
ninety years after Aggeus and Zacharias. Malachias is thus
the last of the prophets. The book seems to have been occasioned by the decay of religious fervour among the priests.
Whether the Temple worship had been steadily growing
colder since the death of Josue, the devout High Priest of
Aggeus's time, or whether it was merely during the absence of
Nehemias in Persia (431-424) that things had got slack we do
not know, but certain it is that Nehemias's second spring
proved a landmark in the history of Juda's oft-repeated cleans-
ings, and it is as likely as not that it was during the loose
years preceding this that Malachias wrote. Farrar puts it elo-
quently: 'In 424 B.C. Artaxerxes died, and the return of
Nehemiah to his office led to strenuous measures of reforma-
tion which perhaps put an end to the laxity and godlessness
which called forth this last flush in the sunset of Hebrew
prophecy.'[10]

On a previous showing the Prophecy of Malachias can quite
definitely be put among the 'burdens' rather than among the
'oracles' or 'words': in parts it is vitriolic. To run one's eye
down the divisions and sub-divisions into which the commentators have cut the text is to stifle the hope that with the
last of the prophets the violence of prophetic ire is spent. We
see heading after heading, like so many Press notices: 'Priests
blamed for neglect of Temple' . . . 'Jews reproached for parti-
san feeling' . . . 'Prophet attacks divorce' . . . 'Impatience,
infidelity, and vain fear reproved' . . . and so on. Malachias
knows how to be stern and he is clearly disgusted with the
Chosen People; in particular is he disgusted with the chosen
priests. If he was a priest himself we can feel for him all the
more; there are few greater trials for a man who is heart and

[10] Farrar, op. cit., p. 224.

soul in his vocation than to stand by while the accepted ideals of his order are being murdered all around him.

The cry which it was chiefly Malachias's business to shout down was the boast that prosperity was one thing and godliness another, and that earthly happiness could perfectly well be attained without reference to the Lord: 'For they that work wickedness are built up' was their cynical judgement on life,[11] 'they have tempted God and are preserved.' Malachias contradicts this sentiment flatly. His denial, it is true, is slightly weakened by the fact that it has to be couched in the terms of 'wait and see if it *is* so sure that the wicked are preserved,' but then it is not the refutation of error that is the prophet's sole concern; or, if it is, the positive doctrine which he holds out with the other hand, the Messianic Hope, will do it for him. 'You shall see the difference between the just and the wicked,' says Malachias, 'between him that serveth God and him that serveth Him not.'[12] And two verses later he tells of the 'Sun of justice' that shall arise, under whose wings shall man find health.[13]

It is not difficult to apprize the state of affairs prevailing in Palestine at the time when Malachias wrote; the hints which can be drawn from the Prophecy itself are reinforced by the Second Book of Esdras. The Temple had of course been finished for half a century or more; the Jews had to a great extent re-established themselves in their own city and money had poured in as in the old days before the Exile. Their one complaint now was that they were still a subject race, despised, suspected, and, except in their financial dealings, ostracised. The religious life, as we have seen, had been watered down for the hundredth time in Hebrew history to the dry, hollow, external system of petty observances and restric-

[11] iii, 15.   [12] iii, 18.   [13] iv, 2.

tions; and even this it was the fashion of the time to ignore
as far as possible, if not reject altogether. So what with the
formalism and ineptitude of the clergy, and the open indif-
ference of the laity—coupled with the affluence and compara-
tively peaceful existence enjoyed by both—it is not surprising
to see how the spirit of worldliness reigned instead of God.

Where Aggeus had to deal with the Jew who was satisfied
to 'take life as he found it without aiming at anything unusual'—the not-very-generous Jew who found it was 'as much
as he could do to keep his feet on the road, never mind about
gazing at the stars'—Malachias on the other hand had to deal
with open querulousness regarding the very need for religion
at all. One could rub along, it was said in effect, very comfortably without. The world had, quite frankly, won; and that
is one reason why the Prophet Malachias is singularly well-
suited to the present time. The devout reader may smile when
he is told that the 'world' is a danger to him, and perhaps in a
sense he is justified: the 'world' of night-clubs and race-meet-
ings has possibly no attraction for him; but is he safe—are
any of us safe?—layman, priest, nun, from the charge that our
standards are being lowered by the 'world'? Has the world
made us satisfied to fail in what we know to be the really
important things of life? That is what is meant by 'worldliness'; it is only another form of what a modern writer has
described as 'rendering to Cæsar the things that are God's.'
And we are all of us liable to that, even if our tastes lie nowhere near the card-room or the turf.

It is not perhaps that we deliberately choose creatures in
preference to the Creator but rather that from very weariness
we stop half-way. We let our cravings for happiness be stilled
by the things of this world instead of pushing them back to
make room for the things of the next. In Malachias's day it

was not that the people had elected to be vicious or that the priests had elected to be lax, but much more probably was it that both priests and people had wearied of waiting for the Lord and had grasped at what was lying at their hands to offer solace. It is the same temptation that attacked the first man, Adam, in the garden; it is the same temptation that attacked the second man, Christ, in the wilderness: to get something at once which it is not in the Father's plan to grant at once. If only we had patience enough, and faith enough, we would lean more upon the words of Christ: 'My peace I give unto you; not as the world giveth do I give unto you,'[14] recognizing well that the world *does give peace*—of a sort. It is the sort, alas, that unfits us for the peace of Christ. We are made for joy, a joy that no man shall take from us,[15] while the joy that the world can give is a joy it can take away again. If we place our joy in anything less than God, the loss of that 'thing' must make us miserable; and even say we never lose it or come near to losing it, there is always the danger that our appetite for the *real* object of our desire will atrophy. If we take all our meals at the confectioner's our taste for solid food is spoiled. We have stopped half-way. We have licked the gilt off the ginger-bread and have no stomach for the rest. No, the good things of this world may not be looked to for complete content—we must all be sufficiently 'mystic' to see as far as that. We place our rest where no storm can possibly disturb it. Troubles come, but it is the surface alone that is troubled; nothing but sin has the power to sadden. As with the mystic, so with the ordinary wayfarer: poverty, war, failures, even the drifting apart of friends, are but the shadows that gather in the folds of the tapestry—to be accounted, if you like, as part of the tapestry's design.

[14] John xiv, 27. [15] John xvi, 22.

Are we not, then, to hold in our hands *at all* the creatures
that are sent us by God? Is not our work, our God-given,
family-supporting work, made *possible* by living in, and mix-
ing with, this evidently-to-be-avoided world? Certainly, God's
creatures must be used; certainly, God's world must be lived
in. It is the business of Malachias to show us how. The question is not how much of me is in the world but how much
of the world there is in me. The mystic, if he is the one
who sees things even dimly as they really are, is surely the best
person therefore to lead us in and out between the obstacles.
It is only the mystic who knows experimentally—though, as
we have seen, inadequately—that God IS WHO IS and that
creatures ARE only in so far as they are related to Him. 'I it am
that is all,' says the Lord to Dame Julian. Furthermore, it is
only the mystic who is sufficiently detached to urge with
Christ that we 'seek first the Kingdom of God and all these
things shall be added.' Far from being despised, the world
is to be admired; it is good; God made it. We it is who have
made it a dangerous place to love too much. We must live in
it nevertheless, and use it wisely. Holy Wisdom, as far as it is
found in us, is nothing more than putting God in the first
place and everything else in its order to Him. (A right conscience is only one that recognizes instantly when this order
has been, or is in danger of being, disturbed.) The 'everything
else' is the world, and on it we do well to tread lightly in our
Godward course, looking at the treasures that lie by the way
even as God Himself looks down at them. 'And your eyes shall
see,' says Malachias, who undoubtedly saw these treasures so,
'and you shall say: the Lord be magnified upon the border of
Israel.'[16]

[16] i, 5.

iii

So much for the doctrine of otherworldliness: that is something positive which Malachias holds out to the mundane. When we come to the negative side of the 'oracle,' the 'burden' side, we see at once that what the Lord wanted Malachias to correct was the abuse of the clerical state. The form which the denunciation takes is peculiar, and suggests incidentally that the priests were not fully aware of the extent of their infidelity.[17] Whether for rhetorical purposes or because he actually entered into debate with his brethren, Malachias is seen to employ the question-and-answer method of attack. So vivid is the dialogue that one suspects more behind the account than meets the reader's eye. There is the hint of quite a lively ecclesiastical synod in Chapters I and II.

The chief evil lay in the incompleteness of the priestly sacrifice. The victims they brought were the leavings instead of the prizes of the flock.[18] The prophet curses 'the deceitful man' who makes a great business of his sacrifice when all the while the oblation is a thing which is 'feeble to the Lord.'[19] Over the shoulders of the moneyed priests whose table he shares, Malachias sees the infinite richness of the priesthood of Christ. 'For from the rising of the sun even to the going down' —how familiar is this text become to us who know the theology of the Mass!—'My name is great among the Gentiles, and in every place there is sacrifice, and there is offered to My name a clean oblation; for My name is great among the Gentiles, saith the Lord of hosts.' And of *this* Sacrifice what is laid upon the table can never be 'contemptible.' Malachias is pointing—did he know it, we wonder?—to the Adequate Atonement of the New Law . . . to the 'mediator of the New

[17] i, 7-10. [18] i, 8. [19] i, 14.

Testament, and to the sprinkling of Blood which speaketh better than that of Abel.'[20]

Though the Mass can never of itself be 'unworthy' as could the Temple sacrifice, it admits, on the part of the priest who offers, of the same insufficiencies that characterized the 'feeble' holocaust. 'Is it not evil?' asks Malachias, 'offer it to thy prince if he will be pleased with it.'[21] The reasoning is practical enough: I have said that your sin consisted in rendering to Cæsar the things that are God's, but if in practice you came to do so, even Cæsar would be disgusted at the meanness of the gift.

Do we of the New Law, in the offering of ourselves, render to God the things that are unfit for Cæsar? Does the priest as he stands at the altar of Christ remember that he is a victim as well as a sacrificer? Does he look upon himself as 'nailed to the Cross with Christ'? Is his blood in the Cup and is his body ready to be broken with the Sacred Host? Listen to the statement of a modern mystic: 'he [the priest] should be willing to shed all his blood for souls in imitation of Jesus on the Cross. Yes, it should go so far as shedding his blood; I saw blood. After ordination he should seek nothing but souls. Earthly honours, human interests, the respect of this world should be nothing to him.'[22] Is this the standard we accept unquestioningly? And yet it should be, *must* be, if the priest is in any sense an *alter Christus*. If the people's unconcern with sanctity astounds the prophet of every age, how much more the unconcern of priests? The priest, if anyone, must be alive to grace. The priest, if anyone, must be prepared to stand in contrast to the world. Uncompromisingly must he

[20] Heb. xii, 24.   [21] i, 8.
[22] Marie Brotel (1819-1888), quoted by Saudreau, *Divine Communications*, Vol. II, p. 192.

pit himself against the sloppy philosophies of his day, the comfort-breeding standards, the specious evasions of principle, the flabby neutralities that smooth over with their silken periods the rougher chapters of the Christian Code. Only the glorious independence that envisages 'blood' and that *really* ranks at naught 'respect of this world,' 'human interests,' 'earthly gains,' can possibly find the voice to shout cant-phrases down. We must be prepared—and especially the priest must be prepared—to bury the *aurea mediocritas*, if need be, out of hand, and to close our ears while we are doing it to the very reasonable protests of our friends. The reaction to the spirit of the world must, if occasion arise, be a violent reaction. We take the Kingdom of Heaven by storm or not at all. We are not passengers. We, in a comfort-loving age (not that other ages are noticeably less so), like to absorb the Gospel spirit gently. We like to think of waking up one day to find our country Catholic. The conversion of England will never come about save by the 'prayer and fasting' of the Gospel of Christ. Neither dialectics, nor politics (nor the eugenics of our fellow-countrymen) shall bring this country to its knees. The gates to the Kingdom open freely, thank God, both as regards the Church on earth and the Church of the Blessed, but not on oiled runners. Nothing but the union of a selfless, mortified clergy with a watching, praying laity can be strong enough to expel 'that kind of devil' whose work it is to cast dust—gold dust for the most part—in the eyes of men.

What has this to do with Malachias? Listen to the prophet's last two verses:

'Behold I will send you Elias the prophet before the coming of the great and dreadful day of the Lord. And he shall turn the heart of the fathers to the children, and the heart of the children to their fathers; lest I come and strike the earth with anathema.'

The direct implication of this passage is clearly to the effect that the Chosen People must ultimately return to the Lord, and that this will effect the reconciliation between the 'children' and the patriarchs, 'whose hearts for many ages have been turned away from them, because of their refusing to believe in Christ' (Challoner). But there is more, surely, to be gleaned from the peroration than that.

It will be noticed that there has been no attempt in the above pages to draw even the roughest charcoal sketch of the Prophet Malachias. There is nothing to show what the man was like. If I were challenged, however, to produce an illustration, I know whom I should choose for a model. I should choose the model whom Malachias himself chooses in the passage just quoted: Elias. It is true that it adds little to the Prophecy to know what its writer looked like, but it is something to have an idea of the type that the writer admired. It is not often that we listen to one prophet speaking of the power of another. But besides hinting at the attitude of Malachias towards Elias, it is perhaps not too fanciful to see in the passage a hint as to what should be our attitude towards 'the Day.' 'I will send to you Elias the prophet,' and we know what kind of man he was. It is to be Elias the Thesbite and his like, then, who 'shall turn the heart'—Elias with his haircloth and fasting, the man of prayer and solitude and poverty, *his* is the lead that must be followed in the manner of our waiting for 'the Day' . . . 'lest I come and strike the earth with anathema.' This is the last line of prophecy in the Old Testament, and not until the preaching of John the Baptist (who 'came in the spirit and power of Elias') was Israel warned again of the coming of the Lord. If the Thesbite is to be the

herald of the Second Coming as the Baptist was the herald
of the First, at least we know now what to expect. 'Do penance for the Kingdom of Heaven is at hand.'[23] If we think to
escape the Messianic Prophets we have it from the lips of
Christ Himself. When Elias comes to 'turn the hearts' of men
it will be something if he finds those hearts prepared to turn.
'Watch, therefore, and pray, for you know not when the time
is.'[24]

[23] Matt. iii, 2; iv, 17.   [24] Mark xiii, 33.